WEST CORNWALL
- REFLECTIONS

To
Uncle John and Auntie Jill,

WEST
CORNWALL
- REFLECTIONS

The lost history of West Cornwall

Enjoy Reading!
Love

ALAN HEARN

First published in Great Britain in 2021

Typeset in AdobeGaramond

Editing, design, typesetting and publishing by UK Book Publishing www.ukbookpublishing.com

ISBN: 978-1-914195-14-3

CONTENTS

ABOUT THE AUTHOR

ALAN HEARN LIVES IN MARAZION, CORNWALL and is a Chartered Surveyor. Over a forty-year career he has worked on a wide variety of property development projects in the United Kingdom, Middle East and Asia. He is Fellow of the Royal Institution of Chartered Surveyors (FRICS), Fellow of the Chartered Institute of Building (FCIOB) and Member of the Chartered Institute of Arbitrators (MCIArb). He worked in the Philippines for more than twenty-five years and is the author of 'The Form of Contract for use in the Philippines', an industry standard document used in property development and refurbishment throughout the Philippines. He is also the author of 'Magellan – A Voyage of life,' which is an historical account of the last voyage of Magellan, the discovery of the Straits of Magellan and the first circumnavigation of the world.

INTRODUCTION

WRITING THIS BOOK HAS BEEN a journey of discovery, which began on a re-visit to our old summer holiday home on Tregonning Hill and has continued to other locations around the coastline of Mount's Bay and the Land's End and Penwith Peninsula.

My love of the county of Cornwall began at an early age when during the late 1960s and early 1970s we always took our annual family holidays at Tregonning House, near the village of Ashton, in West Cornwall. I was just a young boy then, and each year our annual pilgrimage would happen during the two-week factory closedown in July. It was very much a family affair with other aunties, uncles and cousins joining the convoy down to Cornwall. We would be a good group of twelve or so, and for five or six years running we stayed with Mr and Mrs Quiller Collick at their large guesthouse named Tregonning House, situated at the top of Tregonning Hill. There were two houses that they rented out, and these were part of a larger single building, which included their own residence.

In all the time we visited we would stay in the guesthouse facing Mount's Bay to the south-west. Outside there were two ponds stocked with fish, and a small lawned area hedged in on one side with a Cornish stone wall on the other. Being the peak holiday season, the adjacent guesthouse was always occupied by other visitors, and it was never a lonely place in the summer. Tregonning House also operated as a dairy farm, and in addition to the beautiful Guernsey cows, there were dogs and two aggressive swans who located themselves in the larger pond by the entrance of the house. I quickly discovered these two watch guards were best avoided.

Looking back, I still remember vividly the sunny days spent on the beach at Gunwalloe Cove, clambering over the rocks and searching the sea water pools left in their hollows at low tide. Winnianton farm shop by the beach was a treasure trove of sandcastles, seaside games, kites, inflatable toys, and ice cream. These connections are still with me and I cannot visit Gunwalloe or Tregonning Hill without immediately thinking back to those happy holidays. Fortunately, Gunwalloe Cove and Winnianton Farm are now part of the National Trust and remain remarkably unchanged fifty years later, as does Tregonning Hill.

Cornwall is one of Britain's best loved holiday destinations. The rugged landscape, quaint harbour villages, spectacular cliff top views and heritage buildings are just some of the reasons why people love to visit. With over four hundred miles of coastline and an eclectic mix of landscape that combines moorland and sub-tropical plants, the countryside is quite different to other parts of the British Isles. Most people do not realize that Cornwall is almost an island, and is separated in large part from Devon and the English mainland by the river Tamar. When travelling to Cornwall on the Great Western Railway, this separation is highlighted as the train slows down to pass over the Royal Albert Bridge, which was built and designed by the engineering legend Isambard Kingdom

Brunel. The bridge was opened in 1859 by Prince Albert and spans the river Tamar at height between Plymouth in Devon and Saltash in Cornwall.

Throughout Cornwall there is a real sense of times gone by and this is accentuated by the old mine buildings that are dotted around the county. These mine buildings were made of cut granite blocks and consisted of an engine house, rectangular in plan and several storeys high, with a tapering circular chimney stack, between seven to twelve metres tall. Abandoned now, they sit amongst the countryside and hills with a distinctive presence of their own, although many are gradually falling into terminal disrepair. At sunset on a fine day, when the sun is low on the horizon, these lonely granite shells are beautifully silhouetted against a golden amber sky.

Now that I live in Cornwall, I pass by the village of Ashton and Tregonning Hill quite regularly and can't but think back to the holidays with Mr and Mrs Quiller Collick when I see the Tregonning Hill House. It was on a recent birthday that I decided to mark the day with a trek up and across Tregonning Hill, together with a visit to Gunwalloe Cove. There were a few of us and we parked in the village of Ashton and walked up the bridle way towards Tregonning Hill House. The views opened up as we slowly ascended the hill, and provided a good excuse to rest for a while and soak up the scenery. It was a bright day with blue skies and patchy cloud, and visibility was clear to the horizon. I scanned the view south over towards Mount's Bay looking for familiar landmarks, guided by the location of St Michael's Mount, which sits prominently in the bay. As we reached the summit and approached the house, I savoured those happy memories. I realised that it had been thirty years since my last visit, and while I had passed Tregonning Hill many times and seen then hill in the distance, I had not actually been to the house. We walked slowly past Tregonning House and followed the public footpath onto the hill ridge. Not far from the house I saw a memorial plaque located to the left of the pathway. I read the text and was intrigued by its ending:

'Present-day tranquillity of the hillside belies the hard, dangerous and labour-Intensive working conditions of the past.'

The plaque was placed on the hill near a small quarry which was largely overgrown and covered with vegetation. The hollow had been named the 'Preachers Pit' and the plaque was placed there to commemorate the visits of John and Charles Wesley, who were founders of the Methodist movement. The inclusion of the sentence about the hard, dangerous working conditions of the past inspired me to find out more about the area, its mining heritage and where else the Wesley brothers had visited. Within the immediate vicinity there is no shortage of old mine workings and the area of Tregonning is one of the recognised mining districts of Cornwall.

The granite engine houses and chimney stacks are a reminder of the mining heritage that made Cornwall the third largest industrial area in the United Kingdom during the nineteenth century. Mining provided a mainstay of work for the people of Cornwall, but the industry has always been sensitive to market conditions, and when tin and copper prices fluctuated, or the ore loads had been mined to a point where extraction became unprofitable, then work came to an abrupt halt. There was no social welfare system or safety net for the miners or their families, who often depended solely on the income they had from mining. When the mining work in an area came to an end, bringing with it the conse-quential hardships from a cessation of income, many miners migrated overseas to utilise their skills in foreign mining ventures. There are many Cornish communities abroad, which were established because of this migration, particularly in the United States of America, South America and South Africa.

Many of the granite shells of what were the working mines and their chimney tower stacks were constructed in the nineteenth century. But what is not commonly known is that Cornwall had been mining for thousands of years before this and trading its ore domestically and internationally. There are other landmarks in Cornwall that show us of the life and industry in existence since ancient times, and this 'hidden Cornwall' began to emerge as I travelled around the Land's End and Penwith Peninsula.

Cornwall is a mining location because it is part of the Cornubian Batholith, a large mass of granite rock below southwest England. This huge subterraneous granite rock surfaces at Dartmoor, Bodmin Moor, St Austell, Tregonning, Land's End and the Isles of Scilly. This unique geology has provided the minerals and ore that started and sustained the mining industry in Cornwall, and produced the dramatic landscape of rocky peaks, cliffs and boulders brought to the surface by the movement in the earth's tectonic plates. The term Cornubian is from the Medieval Latin name for Cornwall.

When alloyed together, copper and tin produce bronze. The Bronze Age, particularly in ancient civilisations such as Egypt, predates 3,000 BC and the rapid expansion in the demand for bronze ensured that tin and copper were prized metals, and an important trading commodity. Because of its unique geology, Cornwall had rich deposits of both tin and copper throughout the county, more so than in any other location in Britain.

After my visit to Tregonning Hill I started exploring Mount's Bay and the Land's End and Penwith Peninsula. As I visited these various places it was fascinating to discover connections between different places and between different and seemingly unconnected people. What had started as a collection of individual packets of information began to come together and paint a much larger picture of the history of West Cornwall. Unexpectedly for me, it revealed what is a largely unknown and untold history of this part of Cornwall.

I also wanted to highlight the beauty of West Cornwall, using locations in and around Mount's Bay and on the Land's End and Penwith Peninsula. There is something primal about the hinterland with its granite hills, strange rock formations and giant boulders strewn across the countryside. It is the contrast of these harsh granite surfaces with rich agricultural space inland, or the blue seas and crashing waves against the granite cliffs around the coast, that highlight this unique beauty. Within West Cornwall are the mining districts of St Just and Tregonning, both of which are selected areas of Cornwall included as a UNESCO World Heritage Site.

In addition to its UNESCO recognition as a World Heritage Site, nearly one third of Cornwall is a designated Area of Outstanding Natural Beauty under the National Parks and Access to the Countryside Act 1949. This is all a testament to what many of us already know – Cornwall is a beautiful county.

As I travelled around and researched, one location has led to another as connections and ideas began to form. In looking at these different places, some of them naturally fell into time periods and were best described by treating them collectively in their respective time band. In fact, in grouping these places together in a historical context, another story emerged of how, over time, the population moved from one location on the peninsula to another. This was fascinating to follow and raised many questions to which I have researched possible answers. Consequently, without it being my original intention, this work covers both places and how those places have evolved with time. Within the time context we see the development of the Cornish people, that have lived in this region for thousands of years. There are several questions that present themselves, not least of all about when mining first started in Cornwall, and who were the foreign traders buying the tin and copper?

Studying West Cornwall through the ages has shown key pivotal points in history, which changed the beliefs, direction and fortunes of the indigenous people. These events were often in the form of direct and indirect outside influence including invasions, occupations and defence alliances as well as the influence of several key people who literally changed the course of history for this area. By looking back and reflecting, we can now see the impact these events had on the ancient people of West Cornwall.

As far as possible I have only referred to places, buildings and ancient monuments that can still be seen in the present day. There is nothing theoretical about the places described and photographed, but their significance in a historical context does give pause for reflection and I have offered some of my thoughts.

Cornwall drew me in with its ancient monuments, mines, historical characters and stories of a bygone age. When looking back in time, it is a fact that the further you look the less certain you can be of context and meaning. In those situations where details are scarce, I have raised a number of observations and leave any conclusion open to the interpretation of the reader.

The book is entitled 'Reflections' and that is really what is intended – to reflect on the places that we can still see, their history and place in time and what they tell us about the people who built them and lived there.

The words of that plaque remained with me on my travels, *Present-day tranquillity of the hillside belies the hard, dangerous and labour-intensive working conditions of the past.'* It seemed such a key observation as I travelled in all weather, to some of the more remote parts of the Land's End and Penwith Peninsula. The rugged landscape in bleak conditions contrasted dramatically with the blue sea and cliff top views in the summer. How sad it was for generations of miners to be consigned to spending most of their working life underground in dark, damp, treacherous conditions. It is not hard to visualize how life must have been in the past for the generations that lived on this fascinating granite outcrop.

TREGONNING HILL AND TREGONNING HILL HOUSE

OUR JOURNEY BEGINS AT TREGONNING HILL, and since my first revisit a few years ago, I have returned a number of times. There is something special about the hill, which you can sense when walking across the summit. Being at elevation above the surrounding countryside and feeling the wind sweeping over the exposed ridge is part of it, but there is something more, something intangible. Perhaps the answer lies in the stillness of the verdant landscape below – it seems so quiet, unchanged and peaceful.

Located a few miles west of Helston, Tregonning Hill is just to the north of the small village of Ashton. At one-hundred-and-ninety-four metres above sea level it is not especially high, but the uninterrupted views to the coastline and sea level give a height contrast that makes it impressive. The hill has a natural ridgeline that traverses south-east to north-west, and as you walk from one side to the other different views open up over the valleys and plains below. The small villages and individual farmsteads stand out, as do the granite mine houses with their chimney stacks. The extent of the ridgeline is defined by two points – on the south-east side is Tregonning Hill House and on the north-west side is the Grade II listed Germoe War Memorial. Both locations are visible from miles around and mark the furthest boundaries of the ridge.

To the south of the hill the land falls away to the coastline of Mount's Bay, with St Michael's Mount just offshore from the town of Marazion. Beyond St Michael's Mount on the west side of Mount's Bay is the harbour village of Mousehole. As I turned my gaze along the southern coastline towards the east, I followed the line of hills above Perranuthnoe, Praa Sands through to Rinsey Cove and the harbour town of Porthleven.

To the west of Tregonning Hill is the beginning of the Land's End and Penwith Peninsula, which rises up at elevation in the distance. From the Germoe War Memorial the north coast is visible between Lelant and Hayle. Lelant harbour was once a major port for sea travellers landing on the north Cornish coast, and I was later to find out a significant connection between this port and Tregonning Hill.

Looking back towards east Cornwall it is possible to see Carn Brea near Redruth on a clear day. This is another important hill, which stands out for miles around with the Bassett Monument situated on its highest point. On the summit of Carn Brea was once an ancient settlement with its own fortifications.

These views from Tregonning Hill made it strategically important in the past to the people that lived in the area. Long sight lines and a 360-degree panorama provided an ideal lookout point to guard against intruders coming inland from the coast, and to keep watch on movement in and out of the peninsula.

Some of the richest mines in Cornwall were close to Tregonning Hill, and it was at one time the centre of mining activity in the district. Now covered in green vegetation, the hill blends into the surrounding landscape and makes it appear as any other rolling hill in the Cornish countryside. But this hill has a unique history: it was once the seat of a Castle and defensive Hill Fort, and later became the scene of one of the most important discoveries for Cornwall, one that bears economic significance even to this present day.

In the time we holidayed at Tregonning Hill I can only recall a few occasions where we walked across the hill ridge that runs for half a mile or so from Tregonning Hill House in the south to the Germoe War Memorial at its most northern point. We knew that there were disused mines, and even at a young age I recognised that to stray from the footpath was unwise with steep falls partially hidden by undergrowth. Apart from the Germoe War Memorial, I was unaware of any other sites of significance upon the hill. It was therefore a surprise to me while walking across Tregonning Hill on my revisit that I saw a memorial stone, which had inscribed:

WILLIAM COOKWORTHY 1705 – 80

*This stone commemorates the 300ᵗʰ anniversary
of the birth of William Cookworthy, a Plymouth
Quaker Chemist, who discovered China Clay at
Tregonning Hill in 1746.*

The stone was put in place in 2005, some thirty years after my earlier walks across the hill ridge, and provided an explanation to the open cast mining on the east side of the hill. I was naturally curious to find out the history of the discovery by William Cookworthy, and the extent of the mining in the area.

China clay was originally an imported product from China, where it was mined in a village named Gaoling near Jingdezhen in the Jiangxi province. The village name Gaoling is the root of the word Kaolin, which is the technical term for the mineral that is known as china clay. China clay is a form of decomposed granite, and the technical term given to this process is Kaolinization, which occurs when the granite has weathered in wet conditions and broken down over time.

The key component in the production of fine china and porcelain, china clay is a soft white coloured granite that could be crushed into a fine powder and used in a slurry. The versatility and value of this product inspired Englishman William Cookworthy to search for kaolinite deposits closer to home.

William Cookworthy was born on April 12,1705, in Kingsbridge, Devon. He was the first of seven children, and his mother Edith was from St Martin-by-Looe in east Cornwall. A Quaker minister, William Cookworthy had served his apprenticeship as a pharmacist, which appears to be where he became fascinated with the techniques and materials used by the Chinese in making fine porcelain. His searches had brought him to Cornwall, and in 1746, aged forty-one, he discovered china clay on Tregonning Hill.

There were several established mines nearby, notably the Great Works Mine, which sits between Tregonning Hill and Godolphin Hill. These mines were using clay from Tregonning Hill to make bricks for the mine chimneys and furnaces. It was on a visit to the area that William Cookworthy observed the material used in the brick manufacture and this provided the lead he was looking for. He went up Tregonning Hill and found a substantial kaolinite load on the south-east side of the hill.

The discovery of china clay enabled the production of English porcelain and allowed it to compete with imports from China. Over the years the clay was used in a variety of applications including paint, plastic, rubber and high-quality paper.

An operation was set up on Tregonning Hill to mine the china clay and William Cookworthy transported the product to the nearby port of Porthleven, just a few miles south of the mine site. From Porthleven harbour, the china clay was shipped to Plymouth where it was processed and used in the production of porcelain. William Cookworthy later established a company called Plymouth Porcelain, which manufactured fine china in Plymouth, before the factory moved to Bristol. After William Cookworthy's death in 1880, the Bristol factory was sold and moved to Staffordshire, an area synonymous with pottery and fine china.

On Tregonning Hill, the sides of the china clay mine are still visible, and while the undergrowth and vegetation has overgrown the bulk of the excavation, it does not hide the cut back into the side of the hill. Clay mining continued in the area until the late 1800s with census records recording clay miners in the village of Ashton up to the 1891 census.

The legacy of the discovery of china clay has been long lasting and Cornwall still exports china clay out of Fowey on the south Cornish coast. Far larger quantities of china clay were discovered in the St Austell district and this became the epicentre of china clay mining in Cornwall. The landscape in St Austell and the surrounding area bears testament to many years of mining. There is a pyramid of china clay tailings just to the north of St Austell, which stands out like a beacon above the city. One of the disused clay quarries at Bodelva is now the site of the Eden Project with its massive rainforest and Mediterranean Biomes.

The improvement to the Cornish economy due to the discovery and mining of China Clay was evident very quickly. On a visit to St Austell on Monday, September 10, 1787, John Wesley described the journey 'as travelling through a swiftly improving country'. The journal footnote advises that this was 'Owing to the discovery of china clay in the district, in 1768, by Mr. Cookworthy, a Plymouth Quaker.'

In the past the Kaolin from St Austell was mined, processed and transported a short distance to Charlestown Harbour, where it was shipped around the world. Many years later a dedicated china clay loading facility was installed on the edge of the river Fowey, not far from the harbour town of Fowey. A rail line connects to the loading facility and the china clay is brought in by train. For many years English China Clay operated a processing facility on the edge of nearby Par beach close to the Carlyon Bay golf course.

Wheal Martin, the world's only china clay museum, is on the outskirts of St Austell and gives a fascinating look at how china clay was mined over the years. Since the location was once a china clay processing facility, the equipment used and the infrastructure for handling the kaolin and china clay slurry are on display. As I looked around Tregonning Hill I reflected on how still and quiet the place was compared to its former industrial times and how the discovery of china clay on this hill, shaped the course of industry for Cornwall and for the United Kingdom.

The UK is still one of the largest exporters of china clay, which is transported worldwide. In a reversal of the supply chain over the centuries, China now imports china clay from Cornwall, something I think Mr William Cookworthy would have been proud of.

Continuing north over Tregonning Hill from the china clay mine there is a pathway on the left with a sign indicating the entrance to the 'The Preaching Pit'. This is the plaque I quoted from earlier:

The full inscription reads:

The Preaching Pit, a long-disused stone quarry sited here on Tregonning Hill thought to be where visiting Churchmen once preached to the miners of Breage and Germoe – who had a fearsome reputation! It is a fact however, that nearby at Kenneggy Downs in 1743, Charles Wesley preached to 'near a thousand tinners' and that John Wesley visited Breage on 18th August 1750, and again on 10th September 1765, when he recorded in his diary 'I preached at Breage . . .' Present-day tranquillity of the hillside belies the hard, dangerous and labour-intensive working conditions of the past.

The Preaching Pit was a site used for the celebration of Whit Sundays by the local Methodist churches for over one hundred years, and was also used by congregations and preachers who came together to celebrate special occasions and to recall the visits to Cornwall of John and Charles Wesley.

In 1743 just a few years before William Cookworthy made his discovery of china clay at Tregonning Hill, John Wesley, accounted as the leader of the Methodist movement, visited Cornwall for the first time. This was to be the first of over thirty separate visits to Cornwall during a forty-six-year period. John Wesley had initially visited with his brother Charles Wesley, the renowned hymn writer in 1743, and it was John Wesley who had continued the visits well into his later life, with his final visit being at the then remarkable age of eighty-six. For most of his life, he travelled across the county by horse, later by horse and chaise, going from place to place, and often speaking at three or four different locations in one day.

In 1880 the Cornishman Newspaper reported the annual custom of the Ashton Free Church Sunday scholars to walk up Tregonning Hill to the old amphitheatre and hear a sermon.

It is not known if John Wesley ever stood in the Preaching Pit, but he kept a detailed journal of the places he visited, and spent a considerable time in the immediate area. The journal records multiple visits to St Ives, Marazion, St Hillary, Goldsithney, Ludgvan, Helston, Hayle, Gulval, Penzance and Redruth. Given that he made over thirty visits to Cornwall, he would have been very familiar with the area.

The journals of John Wesley record his visits to the village of Breage, which is in the shadow of Tregonning Hill and just along the road from the village of Ashton. His journal notes a further visit to Breage on September 5, 1755, which is not recorded on the marker to the Preachers Pit, and that from Breage he set off on horse to Newlyn. He also preached at a location near Breage called Penhale, which is at the foot of Tregonning Hill. These visits and journeys would have brought him past Tregonning Hill and close, if not through, the village of Ashton.

In looking at West Cornwall across the ages, this book includes a further account of John Wesley's visits to West Cornwall, and the impact this had on the local population. Using his journals and other records it is possible to track his movements and engagements when he was in Cornwall, and it seems most probable that John Wesley, given his natural curiosity, would have ridden up to the summit of Tregonning Hill. His diary records exploring the Land's End cliffs on several occasions and a walk to the top of Carn Brea, near Redruth.

On the north-east of Tregonning Hill ridge are the remains of a hill fort that was called Castle Pencair. The natural defences of the hill provided an ideal location to build a defensive stronghold and the stones used in the wall appear to me to have been brought up the hill rather than mined from its summit. The footpath that crosses the ridge passes by the ruins of this hill fort and as I studied the area I could observe that a number of the walls were recognisable. I also saw several circular stone walls which are possibly the remnants of former dwellings.

Castle Pencair would have been in sight of another important hill fort located on Trencrom Hill, just six miles away. Both of these locations had views to the north and south coast and would have been ideally placed to monitor any movement in the area. A section of this land bridge was later named the St Michael's Way, and the route was popular with travellers wishing to cross between the ports of Lelant and Hayle on the north coast and Marazion on the south coast. This short land connection avoided the need to sail around the Land's End peninsula, which could be treacherous with its shoals, rugged shoreline and heavy Atlantic swells.

Castle Pencair and other parts of Tregonning Hill are classified as a Scheduled Monument and protected under the Ancient Monuments and Archaeological Area Act 1979.

As I completed my journey from Tregonning House to the other side of the ridge, I reached the Germoe War Memorial. This Memorial is located on the north side of Tregonning Hill and honours those fallen from the parish in the First and Second World Wars.

1914 – 1918

Ernest Andrew
Leonard Laity
Ernest Richards
Sampson Richards

1939 – 1945

Ervin Andrews
Stanley Johns
William Courtney White

The monument is registered under the War Memorials Trust and looks out across the countryside, with both the north coast near St Ives and south coast at Mount's Bay visible. I have recorded the family names as a tribute to these men who died in the war and to set in context, that for the villages in the Tregonning Hill area, the First World War came at a time when mining had finally come to an end. Miners from Ashton and Germoe had already started to emigrate abroad by the late 1800s, often leaving their families behind. For those who remained, the loss of a son or father in the wars must have been all the more keenly felt.

There is a small bench seat by the memorial, which looks west. I found it peaceful to sit and contemplate the history of this hill, while viewing the surrounding countryside, and to see the small villages and remains of the nearby mines. There is a real sense of the past in this location and the views of the hills, valleys and bay are seen now, as they would have been by previous generations. That nature has returned to this once highly industrialised area was highlighted by a squirrel who had climbed to the top of the memorial and was quietly watching, not expressing any intention to move on.

On top of Tregonning Hill is a separate scheduled monument humbly recorded as 'Round cairn 225m NW of Tregonning Hill House,' by the Ancient Monuments, UK's online database. Cairns are stone monuments often used for burial and this particular round cairn is believed to date back to the bronze age. These monuments bear witness to the use of Tregonning Hill over many periods of history.

Tregonning Hill has also been designated a Site of Special Scientific Interest (SSSI) in Cornwall. It is of interest due to its ancient sites and for being one of only a few places in the British Isles where western rustwort grows. Western rustwort is classified as a Livewort plant and is reddish in appearance. It is rare in Britain and is found only in Cornwall where it adapts well to clay soils.

On the side of the hill are the remains of an old settlement believed to date back to the sixth century. This site is of significance as it was possibly a point of refuge for the Irish missionaries and saints that sailed into Hayle harbour in the fifth and sixth century. Suffice to say at this point that there was hostility and extreme violence towards the visitors from the local King, and this led to the survivors taking shelter on Tregonning Hill where they used its existing defences.

The author, antiquarian and Anglican priest Sabine Baring-Gould (1834 – 1924) gives an account of West Cornwall being occupied:

> . . . at the end of the fifth and first years of the sixth century by the Irish from the south, mainly from Ossory. An invasion from Munster into that kingdom had led to the cutting of the throats of most of the royal family and its subjugation under the invaders . . . it was probably in consequence of this invasion that a large number of Ossorians crossed over to Cornwall and established themselves in Penwith – the Welsh spell it Pangwaeth, the bloody headland; the name tells a story of resistance and butchery.

He went on to write that, 'As far as we know, the great body of settlers all landed at Hayle. One large contingent, with Saint Breaca at its head, made at the outstart a rush for Tregonning Hill.'

From Irish Saint Breacca we have the town name of Breage, which is nearby to Tregonning Hill. S. Baring-Gould lamented the lack of historical records of this time, and it seems these were destroyed at the dispersion of the monastic libraries. That part of the Celtic contingent survived is known, and many of the town names and parish church names are from the Irish missionaries and saints arriving at this time. Just in the area around Tregonning Hill are:

Germoe – Named after St Germocus or Germoe, an Irish missionary.

Crowan and its Parish Church St Crewanna's – Named after St Crewena, an Irish missionary.

Sithney – Named after Saint Sithney, an Irish missionary.

Saint Erth and its Parish Church St Erth's – Named after Saint Erc, an Irish Missionary, believed to be the brother of St Uny (Lelant Parish Church).

There are many more towns and churches in West Cornwall named after these missionary saints including St Ives named after St Ia, an Irish missionary. Sabine Baring-Gould made a detailed study and issued several volumes on the lives of saints in Britain. He was multi-talented, an Anglican minister, antiquarian and a prolific author. In addition to his studies he was a hymn writer and wrote *Onward Christian Soldiers*. To the north of Tregonning Hill is Godolphin Hill and the Godolphin Estate. Coincidently, Sabine Baring-Gould's grandfather's name was Rear-Admiral Francis Godolphin Bond, and there may have been a distant link to the Godolphin family. What is known is that Rear-Admiral Francis Godolphin Bond was a cousin of Vice-Admiral William Bligh, a Cornishman, made famous by the mutiny on HMS Bounty in 1749.

Similar remains of an ancient settlement exist on nearby Godolphin Hill and it was apparent to me that these settlements had no immediate access to food or water given the location and dense surrounding flora. Standing within the remains I could only think that these communities valued the safety and protection afforded by the hill's natural defences over convenience, since all water, food and materials for fire would have been sourced from lower down and transported up.

At a lower part of Tregonning Hill towards the village of Godolphin Cross is a large round kiln that was used for firing bricks in the 1870s. The bricks were used locally and also exported through Hayle's harbour to New York. This 'beehive' kiln is largely intact and shows the continuance of work in the area even after the local tin industry began to falter. The river Hayle flows close to the Godolphin estate, providing a water connection to the harbour.

Tregonning Hill House is on the south side of Tregonning Hill and overlooks the village of Ashton. The house is visible from miles around, and from the house there are spectacular views of the southern peninsula from the Helston area down to Mount's Bay.

The original building on this site dates back to the Napoleonic Area (late eighteenth century) and was built as a look-out and beacon station to warn against invading forces. Invasion by the French or Spanish was a constant threat during this turbulent period, and in fact the Spanish did invade nearby Penzance, Mousehole and Newlyn in 1595, and razed the towns to the ground. Within sight of Tregonning Hill and to the south west, is St Pol de Leon's Church in Paul, which was set on fire during the Spanish invasion of 1595 and had to be rebuilt. Paul is a village just above the harbour village of Mousehole.

Given the strategic location of Tregonning Hill House, a signal fire started on the west point of Mount's Bay could be repeated on Tregonning Hill and witnessed twenty miles away in Redruth within minutes.

Tregonning Hill House remained of strategic importance for many years before passing into private hands and being used as a residence and a farm. From the 1940s until the 1980s Mr Paul Quiller Collick and Mrs

Lydia Mary Collick had a dairy farm at Tregonning House. The names Quiller and Collick are ancient Cornish names and the Collick family had lived in the Ashton, Breage, and Germoe area for generations. I knew nothing of this when I stayed at the house all those many years ago.

Arriving at Tregonning Hill House was always an event to be celebrated after a tortuous journey from Buckinghamshire to Cornwall in the peak of summer. There were no motorways then, and the regular traffic choke points at Oakhampton and Tiverton were a familiar welcome as we passed through Devon. Over the years the family devised new tactics to combat the traffic, including leaving in the middle of the night, and we would sometimes arrive just after dawn.

I wanted to find out a little more of the couple who hosted us in Cornwall and started to research their family history. I was able to see from gene-alogy records that John Collick (1829 – 1874), Paul Quiller Collick's grandfather, was a tin and copper miner working one of the mines near Germoe, while he lived in Ashton. Probably due to the harsh work-ing conditions and unhealthy environment within the mines he had passed away at the age of forty-five, leaving a widow, Amelia, and ten children.

Edwin Collick (1857 – 1937), the son of John Collick, and the uncle of Paul Quiller Collick, emigrated in 1880 to Ispheming Michigan in the USA. He stayed with Stephen and Sarah Collick, an uncle and aunt, and worked locally in the mines. Edwin stayed in Ispheming for some years before moving to Ironwood, one hundred miles west, where he worked as a head electrician on the mines in the Gogebic area. Both locations were on the south side of Lake Superior. Edwin's younger brothers, Alfred Collick (1859 – 1938) and John Collick (1852 – 1920), followed in his footsteps and emigrated to the mining town of Ishpeming, where they stayed and made it their base.

Over time a term evolved for the Cornish who had settled abroad, and they became known as Cousin Jacks. Perhaps that was due to family networks helping other relatives move out of Cornwall. For the three brothers, Edwin, Alfred and John Collick, their departure from Ashton was out of economic necessity after their father had passed away, and because the mines in the area began to falter. I don't know if Paul Quiller Collick was aware that in addition to three uncles in Michigan he also had twenty-one first cousins. Another cousin from the village of Ashton, Alfred Collick (1885 –1956) emigrated to Silver Bow, Butte, Montana, which was renowned for its huge copper deposits. Alfred died in Butte unmarried and seemingly with no other family members with him. The Cornish communities overseas were close knit and Edwin Collick's son, also Edwin, married Mary Stevens, whose mother was born in Sancreed, less than fourteen miles west of Ashton.

Emigration became commonplace for Cornish miners as mines closed or ran down. Based on census records for the Ashton area this seems to have happened sometime after the 1881 census. In the 1891 census the records for Ashton have multiple entries stating 'Husband miner abroad' next to the family entry. If this situation was so prevalent in a small village the size of Ashton it would have been on a huge scale across the county.

Paul Quiller Collick's father, also Paul Collick (1868 – 1947), took up farming and was recorded in the 1911 census for Ashton as having his own account (farm). It was the farming profession that Paul Quiller Collick continued with successfully, allowing him to purchase Tregonning Hill House. The middle name Quiller was almost certainly a reference to the Cornishman Sir Arthur Quiller Couch (1863 – 1944). Sir Arthur Quiller Couch edited and helped compile the Oxford Book of English Verse 1250 – 1900, and was appointed Professor of English Literature at Cambridge University. A memorial plaque to him is displayed on the long wall within Truro Cathedral.

The Collick family had connections with St Breaca Parish Church in Breage, and the village of Ashton is within the parish of Breage. The Collick family history overlaps in time with the Godolphin family in the 1700s, and the nearest parish church to the Godolphin estate was also St Breaca. The Collick family on both the maternal and paternal sides were closely tied with Tregonning Hill and copper, tin and china clay mining in the area. It is possible that at some point they either worked in a Godolphin mine, or in one where the Godolphin family had an interest. Although connected to St Breaca Parish Church in Breage, one of the Collick family marriages is recorded as having taken place in nearby St Uny Church, Lelant.

Mr Paul Quiller Collick had a very strong Cornish accent and was a man of few words it seemed to me. Both he and his wife Mary were extremely hard working, running their working dairy farm and the sea-sonal holiday let business. The dairy was another attraction for me, and I would wake up early so that I could see the cows coming in from the fields and being milked first thing in the morning. Mrs Mary Collick was a friendly and kind lady, who despite being so busy always made time for guests at the house.

Given the geology of the hill and limited pastureland the dairy farm had only a dozen or so cows, and all of these cows had names. When milking time came the cows would be called into the cow shed. All the names of the cows ended in 'bell' and I remember Copperbell, Goldenbell and Ladybell as a few of the names amongst them. The cows were all from the beautiful golden Guernsey breed and produced a full cream milk that was placed into churns and collected before mid-morning by the local milk distributer.

They were happy times and a few photos survive of our holidays there. I have one particular picture of me with my father in the garden by the pond. Sadly, he passed away in 1999.

Around 1983 I was on holiday in Cornwall and did drive up to Tregonning Hill House. I caught a glimpse of Mrs Mary Collick out on the patio. I wish I had spoken to her, but she seemed busy and I wasn't sure she would remember me. About four years later I was there again and did call in with Maria, my wife, and had tea with Mr Paul Quiller Collick, who had moved into one of the former guesthouses. Sadly, Mrs Mary Collick had passed away on January 12, 1986, and I regret to this day not having spoken to her on my earlier visit. By then Mr Paul Quiller Collick was eighty-two and while he had lost none of his character, he had been through a period of illness. I found out later that he passed away on January 31, 1993, at the age of eighty-eight.

I look back fondly on the couple who worked so hard to keep the farm and holiday home business going on a daily basis. I don't think they had much time for holidays and were restricted by the farm work for opportunities to be away. Despite the setbacks for the Collick family, that drove a number of them to seek work overseas, I think that it was a great family achievement to own the house that generations of them would have looked up to as they made their way from the village of Ashton to the nearby mines.

When I am in the area I can always orientate myself by scanning the landscape for Tregonning Hill, which is visible from multiple vantage points around West Cornwall.

GODOLPHIN HILL AND THE GODOLPHIN ESTATE

THE GODOLPHIN ESTATE IS close by to where I now live. Godolphin House is just a short drive away through the village of Goldsithney and on through the leafy woodlands. The National Trust own and administer the house and grounds, and after parking in the entrance car park, there is a short walk through the woods to the reception area. In April and May the woodland floor is carpeted with bluebells, which makes it such a beautiful place to visit and walk.

Within the grounds of the Godolphin Estate, and located less than one kilometre to the north of Tregonning Hill is Godolphin Hill, the summit of which is at one-hundred-and-sixty-two metres above sea level. Both of these hills are formed from granite and are part of the Cornubian Batholith.

While I had been a regular visitor to the house and gardens, I decided to climb Godolphin Hill shortly after my re-visit to Tregonning Hill.

Godolphin Hill is not visible from the gardens as a meadow slopes up behind the house, obscuring the view of everything behind. I started the walk by the National Trust reception area and made my way up the meadow behind Godolphin House. This was a gentle climb and on reaching the top of the meadow I passed through a short pathway. Towards the end of this path I passed several disused mine shafts that had been protected by stone walls and signposted. Then, at the end of this pathway the hill comes fully into sight. To the left of the footpath is Tregonning Hill and between the two hills is a valley. Situated at a high point in the valley is the old granite engine house and chimney stack of the Great Work Mine. The public footpaths are well-connected and I later discovered it was possible to walk from Godolphin Hill, past the mine and then up to the summit of Tregonning Hill.

As I continued up Godolphin Hill there was a fork in the footpath, and at this junction I saw a granite stone set into the ground on which was inscribed:

THE MAJOR BEQUESTS OF MRS HILDA
PARKER AND A. L. ROWSE C.H. AND
THE GIFT OF DAVID TREFRY ENABLED
THE NATIONAL TRUST TO BUY THE
GODOLPHIN ESTATE IN 1999

Having lived at one time near St Austell, I was well aware of Arthur Leslie Rowse, who was a Cornishman born on December 4, 1903, in Tregonissey, St Austell. He was in the choir at St Austell Parish Church as a youth, and in later life he ran unsuccessfully as an MP for Penryn and Falmouth. Outside of politics he went on to become a prolific author, poet and Elizabethan historian. The C.H refence after his name is for the Order of the Companions of Honour, to which A. L. Rowse was

27

appointed in the Queen's New Year's Honours' list of 1997. He lived in Cornwall near Mount Charles, St Austell, and later bought a beautiful property called Trenarren, which is on the Blackhead Peninsula near Pentewan (Pentewan is between Charlestown and Mevagissey on the south Cornwall coast) His bequest was made in the year of his death, which was on October 13, 1997.

The walk from the house to the top of Godolphin Hill is challenging, but not overly difficult and the views from the summit make it a very rewarding hike. On the summit of Godolphin Hill there are the remnants of an ancient settlement, consisting of a fortified enclosure and six stone circles thought to have once been dwellings. These remains are believed to date back to the Bronze Age and are made up of substantial sections of granite, which were most likely mined lower down the hill and brought to the top with great effort. The remains would have been an impressive fortified settlement with views similar to Tregonning Hill. Apart from the established footpaths, any attempt to climb Godolphin Hill is limited by the dense natural ground cover.

Godolphin Hill is part of the Godolphin Estate, and the National Trust first purchased the fifty-five-acre estate in 1999, and in 2007 completed the purchase of Godolphin House.

Godolphin House was the ancestral home of the Godolphin family and stone mined from Tregonning Hill was incorporated into its construction. Elements of the property date back to the 1500s and may be even earlier since the family were living in the area from the 1300s. The dining room ceiling is said to have been carved from the remains of a Portuguese boat, the Santo Antonio, which sank in Mount's Bay in 1527.

The Godolphin family name is an ancient one and their connection to West Cornwall and the Isles of Scilly is longstanding. The name

Godolphin was arrived at through several changes over time; in 1166 the estate was named Wotolla and later changed to Godholkan. This name is believed to have been formed from the Cornish words 'goodh' and 'olcan' meaning 'tin stream'. At some point in time after 1166, and before the end of the 1300s, the words merged to its current form 'Godolphin'.

Much of the present structure dates back to the seventeenth century and it has been renovated extensively in the last century. The hereditary line of the Godolphin family came to an end in the late 1700s and the title passed to the Duke of Leeds. The Leeds family were based in nearby Leedstown, just a few miles from the Godolphin Estate. However, it seems the Duke, subsequent Dukes and the Leeds family had little interest in Godolphin. While the house and estate continued to operate with staff, the house fell into dilapidation and the property was eventually sold in 1920 by the 10th Duke of Leeds.

Godolphin changed hands several times after 1920 until it was purchased by the Schofield family in 1937. The Schofields spent a considerable amount of time and money in the late 1930s and 1940s renovating and updating the neglected house. Seventy years after they had purchased Godolphin, Mary Schofield completed the sale of the property to the National Trust, who then carried out major conservation works.

The house was a film location for the original television series of Poldark, based on the books of Winston Graham. In the first series, the house is the setting for the fictional Trenwith House, the residence of Francis Poldark.

At Godolphin House, the National Trust have displayed copies of the portraits of Sidney Godolphin, 1st Earl of Godolphin and his son, Francis Godolphin, 2nd Earl of Godolphin. While the bestowing of the earldom in 1706 marked a turning point for the family, it is equally true to say that the Godolphin family had been established over many generations in West Cornwall. One of their closest land-owning neighbours was the St Aubyn family, who had their ancestral home Clowance, in the nearby village of Crowan.

Sidney 1st Earl of Godolphin was baptised on June 15, 1645, in St Breaca, Parish Church Breage, which is a short distance away from the Godolphin Estate. Although the records do not state the place of birth it is most probable that Sidney was born on the Godolphin estate, as his father, Sir Francis Godolphin, had been.

In addition to their own family estate, the Godolphin family had for generations controlled the Isles of Scilly. Sir Francis Godolphin (1540 – 1608), the great grandfather of Sidney 1st Earl of Godolphin, had been the Governor of the Isles of Scilly for over forty years (1568 – 1608) and in 1593 led the development and construction of the Star Castle, on the Isles of Scilly. This impressive structure was part of the fortification works of the British coastline during the war between Spain and England. The Star Castle still exists and is now a popular hotel on the Isles of Scilly. Sir Francis was later made Lord Lieutenant of Cornwall and was succeeded in that post by Sir Walter Raleigh.

Sir William Godolphin (1567 – 1613), the grandfather of Sidney 1st Earl of Godolphin was also Governor of the Isles of Scilly, and like his father Sir Francis Godolphin, was a Member of Parliament. Sir William was also a soldier and an expert on mining, experience he would have gained from the mining on and around Tregonning Hill and Godolphin Hill.

As interesting as the family history is, for me the most intriguing story about the Godolphin family concerns the reputed stay of Charles, Prince of Wales, later to become King Charles II, in the King's Room at the Godolphin estate, and the help the Godolphin family reputedly gave the future King to escape the pursuing parliamentarian forces. Prince Charles was on the run in 1646 following successive defeats for the royalist forces during the English Civil War. The royalists had been pushed further and further west, and finally into Cornwall. Prince Charles did sail from Cornwall to the Isles of Scilly, and stayed there for several weeks before sailing for Jersey, and then onto continental Europe.

I was intrigued to find out whether the story of the Godolphins' help was true.

After the Norman Conquest land ownership was transferred in the twelfth century to those families who were aligned and loyal to William the Conqueror. This ensured that, for a period of time, the loyalties of the landowners were with the crown. The fortunes of the monarch and the major landowners were intertwined, and in West Cornwall the Godolphin family were staunch royalists.

Sir Francis Godolphin (1605 – 1667), the father of Sidney 1st Earl of Godolphin, had followed in his ancestor's footsteps, and was the Governor of the Isles of Scilly and a Member of Parliament. Sir Francis Godolphin was a young Member of Parliament for Helston in 1625, the year King Charles I ascended the throne.

King Charles I believed in his right to rule without interference from Parliament, and there had been tension for some years between the King and the Members of Parliament. These tensions were in part due to the religious views of the King and his marriage in 1625 to Henrietta Maria, a French Princess who was also a Roman Catholic. During the period 1629 – 1640, the King had ruled without calling a Parliament, but was short of funds to expedite all of his plans. In 1641 the King desired Parliament to approve further expenditure for a force to enter Scotland and quell a rebellion. Parliament declined the request, which in turn led to a stand-off and the King taking alternative actions to raise the support he needed.

The King's plans failed, and he was defeated by Scottish forces who then went on to invade Northumbria. All of these events, and the denial by Parliament of the King's requests, led to greater and more acute disputes, that were not able be reconciled.

After the turmoil of Roman, Saxon and Norman invasions of England, there had been a period of relative calm as the Middle Ages came to an end. However, this relative tranquillity was about to be shattered by the advent of the English Civil War. Both Parliament and King Charles I were on a collision course.

The English Civil War had its origin shortly after King Charles I and his armed soldiers entered the House of Commons on the January 4, 1642, to arrest five Members of Parliament. The five members, John Hampden, Arthur Haselrig, Denzil Holles, John Pym and William Strode, managed to escape and avoid capture. However, this was an unprecedented action by any monarch and was the spark that led to a bloody conflict, pitting countrymen against countrymen.

Cornwall as a county was loyal to King Charles I and families such as the Godolphins rallied to support the royalist cause. Together with other Members of Parliament who were allied with the royalists, Francis Godolphin was barred from entering the Houses of Parliament, and representing his constituency.

As testament to this support, the King wrote a letter to the county of Cornwall that was required to be read out in every church:

CAROLUS I REX

A LETTER OF THANKS FROM KING CHARLES I
OF BLESSED MEMORY

*We are so highly sensible of the extraordinary Merits of Our County
of Cornwall, of their Zeal for the Defence of our Person, and the Just
Rights of Our Crown, in a time when We could contribute so little
to our own Defence, or to their Assistance; (in a time, when not only
no Relief appeared, but great and probable Dangers were threatened
to Obedience and Loyalty) of their Great and Eminent Courage and
Patience in their Indefatigable prosecution of their great work against
so Potent an Enemy, back with so Strong, Rich and Populous Cities,
and so plentifully furnished with Men, Arms, Money, Ammunition
and Provisions of all kinds; and of the wonderful success with which
it hath pleased Almighty God (though with the loss of some Eminent
persons) who shall never be forgotten by Us to reward their Loyalty and
Patience) by the strange Victories over their and Our Enemies, in despite
of all humane probabilities and all imaginable disadvantages; that as
We cannot be forgetful of so great Deserts, so We cannot but desire to
publish to all the World, and perpetuate to all time the memory of their
Merits, and Our Acceptance of the same. And to that end, We do hereby
render Our Royal Thanks to that Our County in the most publick and
lasting manner We can devise, Commanding Copies hereof to be Printed
and published, and one of them to be read in every Church and Chapel
therein, and to be kept for ever as a Record in the same, that as long
as the History of these Times, and of this Nation shall continue, the
Memory of how much that County hath merited from US and Our
Crown, may be derived with it to Posterity.*

*Given at our Camp at Sudly Castle
the Tenth of September 1643.*

The original letter had begun with, *To the inhabitants of the county of Cornwall: a letter of thanks from King Charles I of ever blessed memory, dated Sept. 10, 1643 from Sudly Castle.*

The royalists had several initial victories in the Civil War, where their armed forces utilised a distinct advantage of better training and organisation. However, by 1643 Oliver Cromwell and his Ironside forces began to turn the tide and by the time the New Model Army had been formed in 1645 the Royalist cause was in serious trouble.

Following defeats at the hands of the Parliamentarians, royalist forces retreated across southern England. With each defeat the royalist army headed westward – into Somerset, then Devon and finally into Cornwall. The royalists had surrendered Bristol on September 10, 1645, and by February 16, 1646, they had lost the battle of Torrington in Devon. A few months later they lost the city of Exeter.

The fifteen-year-old Charles, Prince of Wales, joined the retreating royalists into Cornwall. It must have been a terrifying experience for the future king as he took in the scale of the defeat, and the acknowledgment that he must prepare to leave the country of his birth. The Parliamentarian forces were closing in and Cornwall was no longer safe. His father, King Charles I, had written to his son advising that in no circumstances was he to be taken prisoner, even if that meant going into exile.

I believe it is highly likely that Sir Francis Godolphin assisted the young Prince Charles while he was in Cornwall. The escape plan had already been hatched and the future king would be brought to the Isles of Scilly, which had for generations been under the control of the Godolphin family. It was a fortified location and provided a formidable defence, separated as it was by the thirty miles of sea from the mainland. We know that Sir Francis Godolphin was a committed royalist, and his brother,

Sidney Godolphin, had died fighting the royalist cause in the battle of Chagford, on February 10, 1642, aged thirty-two.

It is also quite possible that the young Prince Charles stayed at the Godolphin Estate, Parliamentary forces had not yet overrun Cornwall and the Godolphin Estate would have been a perfect location. In nearby Marazion there is a sign on a house by the harbour recording that Prince Charles stayed overnight on March 2, 1646, before leaving for the Isles of Scilly.

Under the protection of its Governor, Sir Francis Godolphin, Prince Charles arrived in St Mary's on March 4, 1646, where he stayed six weeks. Some reports have Sir Francis Godolphin sailing to the Isles of Scilly with the young prince, which I would believe are likely correct. After departing the Isles of Scilly for Jersey, Prince Charles continued to Europe where he remained in exile.

As the parliamentary forces exerted their control over Cornwall the Godolphins had their estate forfeited. However, Sir Francis Godolphin was able to negotiate the estate back in exchange for a peaceful handover of the Isle of Scilly to the parliamentary forces.

On January 30, 1649, King Charles I was executed for treason in London and buried in Windsor Castle. Under Oliver Cromwell, the country was ruled as a protectorate with him as Lord Protector until his death in 1658. Oliver Cromwell's son Richard, given the unfortunate nickname of 'Tumbledown Dick', was not able to continue in the way his father had ruled and resigned after less than one year in office. The mood of the country had changed, and the Prince of Wales was invited back to take up the crown.

Prince Charles returned and was crowned King Charles II at Westminster Abbey on April 23, 1661. Sir Francis Godolphin was invited to the coronation and was knighted the same day. I think this strongly supports the claim that Sir Francis Godolphin helped the young Charles, Prince of Wales escape in 1646. It is fair to say that this was the first opportunity King Charles II had to publicly acknowledge and reward the Godolphin family for the services they had rendered to him. This public recognition of the Godolphin family continued with Sir Francis Godolphin's son, who went on to become Sidney 1st Earl of Godolphin. Sidney was less than one year old when the young Prince of Wales escaped out of Cornwall.

Following the coronation of King Charles II, there then followed a period of persecution for all who had signed the death warrant of his father, King Charles I, and who were collectively referred to as the regicides. Those men that were still alive after the return of the King were all hunted down and executed in horrific circumstances. Even the dead regicides did not escape the wrath of the King Charles II. Oliver Cromwell, who had died in 1658, was exhumed from Westminster Abbey on January 30, 1661, exactly 12 years after King Charles I's execution, and his body was subjected to a posthumous execution in Tyburn, London. His former comrades John Bradshaw, Robert Blake and Henry Ireton also suffered the same fate. Oliver Cromwell's head was placed on a pole and displayed at Westminster Hall for the duration of King Charles II reign from 1661 to 1685.

Sir Francis Godolphin continued as a Member of Parliament for Helston and Governor of the Isles of Scilly. In 1651 the author Thomas Hobbes (1588 – 1679) dedicated his book 'Leviathan', or to give it is full name 'The Matter, Forme and Power of a Common-Wealth, Ecclesiastical and Civil' to Sir Francis Godolphin. The dedication read:

Honor'd Sir

Your most worthy Brother Mr Sidney Godolphin, when he lived, was pleas'd to think my studies something, and otherwise to oblige me, as you know, with reall testimonies of his good opinion, great in themselves, and the greater for the worthinesse of his person. For there is not any ventue that disposeth a man, either to the service of God, or to the service of his Country, to Civill Society or private Friendship, that did not manifestly appear in his conversation, not as acquired by necessity, or affected upon occasion, but inhaerent and shining in a generous constitution of his nature.

Therefore, in honour and gratitude to him, and with devotion to your selfe, I humbly Dedicate unto you this my disclosure of Common–wealth.

Sir Francis Godolphin passed away in 1667 and was buried in Crowan, Cornwall. Crowan was the location of Clowance House, the then seat of the St Aubyn family, who were on the side of the Parliamentarians during the Civil War.

Sidney Godolphin, 1st Earl of Godolphin (1645 – 1712), was twenty-two at the time of his father's death. Four years earlier, on September 28, 1663, he was conferred with a Master of Arts (M.A.) when attending King Charles II in Oxford. He built on the relationship his father had established, studied law in London, and became a Member of Parliament for Helston and later for St Mawes. His brother Henry became the Dean of the rebuilt St Paul's Cathedral in 1707, ten years after it was consecrated. The Dictionary of National Biography records, 'During his tenure of office at St Paul's he greatly thwarted Sir Christopher Wren in his efforts to erect a suitable cathedral.'

Sidney Godolphin 1st Earl of Godolphin served in a number of important roles under four monarchs, Charles II, James II, William and Mary.

He was clearly a very talented man, reaching the heights as Secretary of State, First Commissioner of the Treasury and member of the Privy Council. He was made a Baron in 1684 and an Earl in 1706. He passed away on September 15, 1712 and was buried in Westminster Abbey.

Chalmers General Biographical Dictionary quoted the following: Bishop Burnet said of him 'that he was the silentest and modestest man who perhaps ever bred in court'.

He was also described as 'one of the worthiest men who was employed in that age, and he was a man of the clearest head, calmest temper and the most incorruptible of ministers'.

After the death of Sidney 1st Earl of Godolphin in 1712, the title passed to his son, Francis Godolphin, 2nd Earl of Godolphin (1678 – 1766). Francis Godolphin shared the same name as his grandfather and continued the family tradition of being a Member of Parliament for Helston. Like his father, he was talented and served under several monarchs.

Around 1733, Francis Godolphin purchased a horse named Shami. This thoroughbred horse was foaled in 1724 in Arabia and became known as the Godolphin Arabian and also the Godolphin Barb. He was one of three stallions that founded the modern thoroughbred horse. Shami was a handsome and remarkable horse that sired eight foals and was described as headstrong. His Highness Sheikh Mohammed bin Rashid Al Maktoum, Vice President and Prime Minister of the United Arab Emirates and Ruler of Dubai founded the world's largest horseracing team and named it Godolphin in honour of the Godolphin Arabian. Godolphin's headquarters are in Dubai and has teams training in four continents. There is an annual horse race named the King Charles II stakes and horses from the Godolphin team often feature in it.

Sadly, at the time of Francis Godolphin's death in 1766, his two sons had predeceased him and there was no heir to pass the title on to. As a consequence, the Earldom of Godolphin and Viscountcy of Rialton ended. This was the end of the male bloodline through the two Earls, but there were other male relatives from other lines of the family. The Barony of Godolphin of Rialton passed to his cousin Francis Godolphin, who became the 2nd Baron of Godolphin. However, on his death nineteen years later in 1785, the title became extinct.

It was a tragic end to the Godolphin Earldom, which had lasted just over seventy years and through only two generations. The family had reached its zenith and then, shortly after, had petered out.

The escape of the young Prince of Wales from Cornwall during the Civil War, was a pivotal moment in history. The subsequent reign of King Charles II saw a time of significant change that had far reaching consequences within the United Kingdom and throughout the world. Britain would have been a very different place had the monarchy not been reinstated and the puritanical protectorate continued.

Had the young Prince of Wales been captured, he might have suffered the same fate as his father, and the course of history would have turned out very differently. Instead, his escape and subsequent freedom on the continent kept the royalist flame alight. The invitation to return was a high point for Charles, and a document was set into law that all who had signed his father's death warrant (the regicides) would be subject to punishment, while other parliamentarians who had not signed the warrant would be pardoned of any action arising out of and during the Civil War. The details were contained in 'The indemnity and Oblivion Act' which came into law in 1660.

When Charles returned, he was received with great celebration and adulation both before and during the coronation. However, the period after his coronation turned out to be quite turbulent and this started to change the perception people had towards the reinstated monarchy. There were the twin tragedies of the great plague that began in 1665, and the Great Fire of London 1666, which wiped out most of the capital city. There was also the continuation of the second and third Anglo Dutch wars with the Netherlands, which greatly reduced the capacity of the Royal Navy and impacted international trading.

The release from a puritanical protectorate saw the reopening of theatres and a general increase in trade. Both the sciences and the arts prospered with such notables as Isaac Newton, Robert Boyle, Christopher Wren, Samuel Pepys and Edmund Halley all living through this era. Under King Charles II's reign, London was literally rebuilt from the ashes and work to rebuild the iconic St Paul's Cathedral was started.

In 1660, The Royal Society of London for Improving Natural Knowledge was formed and was granted a Royal Charter by King Charles II in 1662. Scientists had endured some suppression during the protectorate and small groups had met in secret to discuss ideas. The forming of this society, whose lengthy name was later shortened to 'The Royal Society', provided a venue for science to advance, experiments to be carried out and theories to be developed. Robert Boyle (1627 – 1691) was a founding member of The Royal Society and developed his own research on the relationship between the pressure and volume of gas under certain conditions. His findings and conclusions were published and became known as Boyle's Law. Between 1676 – 1679 he worked with a Frenchman, Dennis Papin (1647 – 1713), developing steam apparatus, including one machine known as the steam digester. This work was a forerunner to the advent of steam engines and further work by Thomas Savery (1650 – 1715) and Thomas Newcomen (1664 – 1729) brought the first steam driven engines used to pump water from mines. One of the first mines to trial both the Savery engine and later the Newcomen engine was Wheal Vor in Cornwall. The Godolphin family had an interest in this mine, which lies close to their estate, between Breage and Godolphin cross, in the shadow of Tregonning Hill. At one time Wheal Vor was the richest mine in all of Cornwall and the area was mined over centuries. Nearby, another of Godolphin's mines, 'The Great Work Mine', was said to have been the first mine to trial the use of gunpowder blasting in 1689. It is not surprising that the Godolphin family had access to this new mining technology as Sidney Godolphin, 1st Earl of Godolphin, was a royal favourite and held a succession of important roles. As well as acting as a special envoy for the king in international matters, he was made a member of the Privy Council in 1679 and a Baron in 1684. He had unrestricted access to the King and the King trusted him with the most delicate of matters. In Cornwall, his mining interests continue to grow and expand under this royal sponsorship.

It would be difficult to not see the link between the protection of the young King Charles II in 1746 by the Godolphin family, and their rise in fortunes after the reinstatement of the monarchy. Significantly, the restoration of King Charles II had created a different environment where science could flourish, and as a result of this, scientific breakthroughs were made in many areas. The development of steam driven engines grew out of work undertaken by The Royal Society and its members. One of the derivatives from this innovation was the benefit brought to the mining industry in Cornwall from the early introduction of the new steam driven pumps. This form of pumping allowed the mines to dig deeper for ore and led to the building of the granite engine houses and chimney stacks that we still see today. The early introduction of the steam driven pumps to Cornwall was linked to the Godolphin family, who showcased the pumps at mines they owned outright or where they had some connection. Some years after the introduction of steam driven equipment to the area, Cornwall produced its own engineering genius in the form of Richard Trevithick (1771 – 1833), who grew up watching these early engines near Redruth, before going on to develop high pressure steam engines and the first railway locomotive.

King Charles II was charismatic and often unpredictable; on March 4, 1681 he gave away 45,000 acres of land to William Penn (1644 – 1718), whose arrest in 1670 had led to the infamous 'Bushels Case'. This vast tract of land was in America and made William Penn the largest private landowner in the world. William Penn developed and administered the territory into what became modern Pennsylvania.

The King's unpredictability could work both ways as it did in the case of Henry Vane the Younger. Born in 1613, Henry Vane was the son of Henry Vane the Elder (1589 – 1655), who had been an ambitious man, knighted at the age of twenty-two and rising in rank to become Treasurer of the Household under King Charles I. In his earlier days he had represented Lostwithiel, Cornwall as a Member of Parliament, and was cofferer to the Prince of Wales. Henry Vane the Younger became a puritan during his teenage years and studied in Oxford and in Europe. He then left for America with the puritan migration that was happening at that time, He became the Governor of the Massachusetts Bay Colony, and supported the creation of the Rhode Island Colony, and Harvard College.

He returned to England and was appointed Treasurer of the Royal Navy in 1639. When the Civil War began in 1642, he sided with the Parliamentarians, and later during the Interregnum (the period between the execution of King Charles I in 1649 and the return to England of King Charles II in 1660) he acted as the Government Executive. He worked closely with Oliver Cromwell, although they did not always get on and, eventually, they split. Oliver Cromwell even had Henry Vane imprisoned in Carisbrooke Castle on the Isle of White at one point. Although a prominent parliamentarian, Henry Vane had refused to sign the death warrant of King Charles I and after Oliver Cromwell's death, plotted against the rule of Richard Cromwell. Since Henry Vane had not signed the death warrant of King Charles I he might have expected to be pardoned of any civil war actions. However, he was arrested and imprisoned in the Tower of London prior to the Act coming into force in August 1660. Once the Act was passed there was a petition to King Charles II for clemency, which was granted. However, Henry Vane continued to be kept in the Tower, and his lands and property were seized by the crown, depriving him of the ability to honour his debts. In what seemed an act of vindictiveness, Henry Vane was then moved to the Isles of Scilly in October 1661 where he remained imprisoned and isolated. Sir Francis Godolphin, who had protected the young King Charles II in 1646, was the Governor of the Isles of Scilly in 1661 when Henry Vane was imprisoned there. There seems a sense of retribution in the treatment of Henry Vane, and the choice of the Isles of Scilly for his imprisonment, echoes back to the time King Charles II spent six weeks there while on the run.

Henry Vane was moved back to the Tower of London in April 1662, and subsequently put on trial. He was executed on June 14, 1662, on Tower Hill. The only concession King Charles II made was that Henry Vane would be beheaded, rather than hung, drawn and quartered. The poet John Milton (1608 – 1674) dedicated a sonnet to Henry Vane the Younger.

King Charles II died in 1685 from what appeared to be a stroke. He had refused an Anglican priest on his deathbed, instead requesting his last rites be read by a Roman Catholic priest. While he had been for religious tolerance after the strict puritanical regime prior to his reign, he had never confessed himself to be a Catholic. If he had that would have been the end of his reign and it showed the influence his mother's religion had had on him. King Charles had fathered twelve children with a number of mistresses, but they were considered illegitimate, and therefore were not in line to the throne.

On my frequent visits to the Godolphin Estate, I always replay the scene in my mind when I visit the King's Room and Garden, imagining the future King looking out through the window and wondering what his future might hold. Rumours and old stories often have more than a grain of truth in them and it seems to me, as I stand there, that the future King Charles II really could have been in that very room three-hundred-and-seventy-years ago.

When travelling around the area of the Tregonning and Godolphin mining district, there are numerous granite engine houses and stacks in the fields and countryside. Some are inland and some are on the coast-line, and a walk along the South West Cornish coastal path takes you past Wheal Prosper mine and Wheal Trewavas mine. These two granite engine houses are perched dramatically on the cliff edge with wonderful views out to sea.

One of my favourite mines within this mining district is the Tregurtha Downs Mine, which is within walking distance from Marazion. The three-level engine house and chimney stack have been beautifully pre-served and are now a private residence. I think it is one of the best kept examples of an old working mine within the whole of Cornwall.

Closer to the Godolphin estate and near the village of Carleen are the remains of Wheal Vor, once a huge mining operation covering four-teen hundred acres of ground. Other nearby mines are West Godolphin mine, Wheal Grey mine, Wheel Reeth mine, Trebolence mine and Nancegollan mine. Further away at Praa Sands are the remains of the Sydney Godolphin mine.

Mining has taken place over many centuries and there are numerous mines within the Godolphin Estate or close by. One of these was the Godolphin Mine, which was a copper mine located half a kilometre north-east of Godolphin House. The mine is near the river Hayle and its remains are now buried in a tangle of undergrowth amongst the woodlands. It is never a good idea to stray from footpaths in Cornwall's woodland as there are many unmarked mine shafts, supposedly sealed up, but not maintained.

Higher up on the estate, the Great Work Mine sits between Godolphin Hill and Tregonning Hill, and the engine house and stack are visible from a distance, The mine can be visited, and safety work has been undertaken to seal off the open shafts with metal gratings. The Great Work Mine was a successful and profitable mine and was at peak activity in the nineteenth century. Ore from a smaller mine on Tregonning Hill was also brought to the Great Work Mine for processing.

Mining has taken place in this location for many hundreds of years and employed hundreds of people, even in the sixteenth century. The poet and antiquary John Leland had visited the estate in 1538 and said, 'There are no greater Tynne workes yn al Cornwal than be on Sir William Godolcan's ground.' One report noted that there were over one-hundred-and-forty recorded mine shafts on the Godolphin Estate in 1837.

After the separation of tin from the ore, the tailings or residue crushed rock was taken to a nearby field which became known as the after washes. Here the rock was mixed with water and the slurry run across inclined boards to help separate the heavier particles.

The countryside around the Godolphin Estate is now well established, with mature trees and lush greenery and imparts a sense of serenity, and it always calls to my mind the marker on nearby Tregonning Hill:

> *Present-day tranquillity of the hillside belies the hard, dangerous and labour Intensive working conditions of the past.*

When you walk through the Godolphin estates and Tregonning Hill it is easy to let your mind drift back to a different time in history and remember those generations that built a hill fort on Godolphin Hill and later started to mine the area. The area is steeped in history and the land has for centuries been inextricably linked to the Godolphin family. This family prospered over many generations and left the lasting legacy that we see today. How wonderful, that the story of all these generations is kept alive by the National Trust and others.

Sidney Godolphin
1st Earl of Godolphin
(1645–1712)

Francis Godolphin
2nd Earl of Godolphin
(1678–1766)

The Godolphin Barb or
The Godolphin Arabian
(c. 1724–1753)

From Under the Sea, 1864

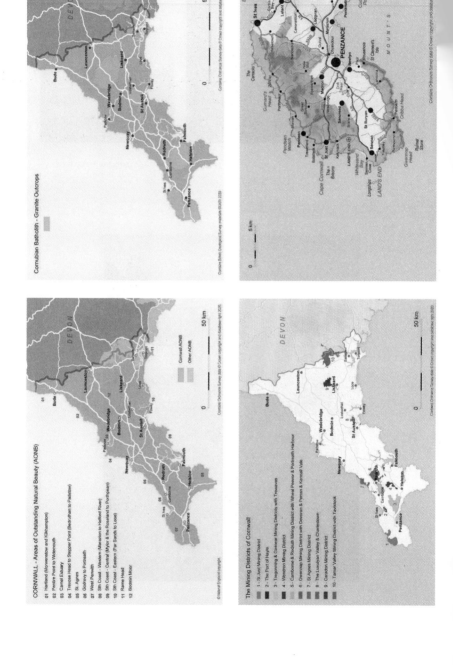

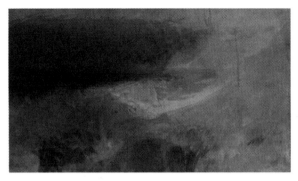

*Jospeph Mallord
William Turner –
Land's End*

*J.M.W. Turner –
St Michael's Mount*

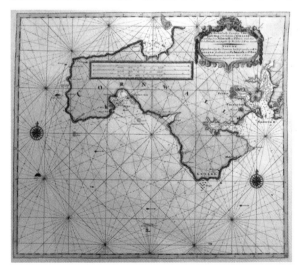

*G. Van Keulen
Map of Cornwall.
Published 1728*

West Cornwall

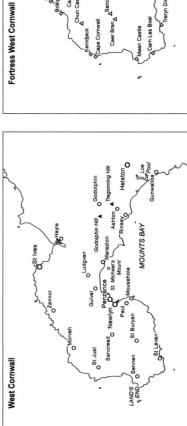

St Ives
Hayle
Zennor
Morvah
Guival
Ludgvan
St Just
Sancreed
Newlyn
Penzance
St Michael's Mount
Marazion
Paul
Mousehole
St Buryan
LAND'S END
Sennen
St Levan
Godolphin Hill
Godolphin
Tregonning Hill
Ashton
Rinsey
Helston
Loe Pool
Gunwalloe
MOUNTS BAY

Fortress West Cornwall

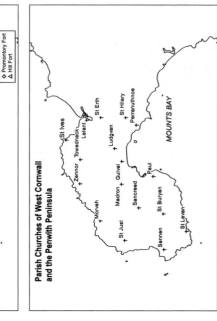

Gurnard's Head
Bosigran Castle
Castle An Dinas
Chun Castle
Kenidjack
Cape Cornwall
Caer Bran
Maen Castle
Carn Les Boel
Treryn Dinas
Carnsew
Trencrom
St Michael's Way
Lescudjack
Sancreed Beacon
St Michael's Mount
Castle Pencair
MOUNTS BAY

◇ Promontory Fort
△ Hill Fort

Ancient Sites on the Penwith Peninsula

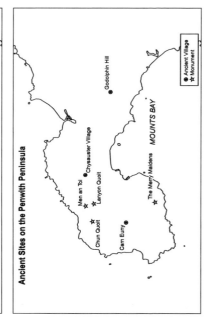

Men an Tol
Chysauster Village
Lanyon Quoit
Chun Quoit
Carn Euny
Godolphin Hill
The Merry Maidens
MOUNTS BAY

● Ancient Village
★ Monument

Parish Churches of West Cornwall and the Penwith Peninsula

St Ives
Zennor
Towednack
Lelant
St Erth
Ludgvan
St Hilary
Perranuthnoe
Morvah
Madron
Gulval
St Just
Sancreed
Paul
Sennen
St Buryan
St Levan
MOUNTS BAY

Map Marketing

St Michael's Mount

POETRY HAS ALWAYS BEEN important to me with lines and rhythms sometimes coming to mind unprompted. Once the line is in, I can spend weeks or months developing the rest of the verse. We are fortunate to live opposite St Michael's Mount and see it through all seasons. The following verses developed over a period of time:

> *St Michael's Mount rises up from the seas,*
> *crowned with a castle above the green trees.*
> *An elegant and aged fortress rock,*
> *with a sheltered harbour for ships to dock.*
>
> *Separated from the headland by time and tide,*
> *Its beauty a reason for national pride.*
> *Karrek Loos Y'n Koos is its Cornish name,*
> *'grey rock in a wood' its English refrain.*

Sitting prominent in Mount's Bay,
The tides form an island twice a day.
Drawing visitors from far and wide,
crossing the causeway at low tide.

A civil war fortress in times gone past,
a royalist stronghold until at last.
Parliamentary forces won the day,
after laying siege at Mount's Bay.

St Michael's Mount is an ancient rock that once formed part of the ancient fort defences in West Cornwall. It is visible from Trencrom Hill Fort, which is located to the south of St Ives and is also in sight of Tregonning Hill and Godolphin Hill.

Named after the Archangel Saint Michael, St Michael's Mount has historical links with Mont Saint-Michel in Normandy, France, and was once a Benedictine Priory. During the Middle Ages there were ties with France, although these were dampened during the Hundred Years' War between England and France, during the period 1337 – 1453.

The mount was originally surrounded by woodland and locals report that when there is a very low tide in Mount's Bay the remnants of trees stumps, now covered by the ocean, can be seen. This gives understanding to St Michael's Mount's Cornish name, which means 'Grey Rock in the Wood'. In other words, it was at one point part of the peninsula.

St Michael's Mount was used as a fortress in the first English Civil War and royalist forces held out against the Parliamentary forces. A siege ensued and the royalist forces under Sir Francis and Sir Arthur Basset finally surrendered on April 23, 1646.

Colonel John St Aubyn (1613 –1684) was a Parliamentarian during the Civil War and was involved with the siege of the Mount in 1646. The following year in 1647 he was made Captain of St Michael's Mount, which was then used as a prison for a time. In 1659 he purchased St Michael's Mount from the Basset Family, whose fortunes had declined as a result of their support for the royalist cause.

According to the cartographer and antiquarian John Norden (1547 – 1625) in his work, *A Topographical And Historical Description of Cornwall (1728)*, the steep and most craggie torr was called sometime *Dinsol* or in the Cornish language *Careg Cowse*. He attributes the construction of much of the buildings at the top of the mount to William Moriton (Count of Mortain and Third Earl of Cornwall (bef. 1084 – aft. 1140) who was a nephew of William the Conqueror.

In what must have been a major event at the time, John St Aubyn, the Parliamentarian, married Catherine Godolphin on March 29, 1637. Although this was five years before the outbreak of the Civil War, Catherine was a third cousin of Sir Francis Godolphin the royalist, and tensions between King Charles I and Parliament were already high. The marriage took place in Exeter, Devon rather than Cornwall, and this may have been because of the diverse sympathies on both sides of the family. When the Civil War broke out, Sidney Godolphin, also a third cousin to Catherine, was killed in battle fighting the royalist cause in Devon in February 1643.

The marriage does appear to have been a success and the couple had ten children. Catherine passed away in 1662 and John St Aubyn outlived his wife by twenty-two years. They were both buried in the St Aubyn ancestral home, at Clowance Estate, in nearby Crowan.

I have visited the estate several times, and there is a sign at Clowance House which provides further details on the history of the house and the St Aubyn family:

The St Aubyns came over to England with William the Conqueror. Clowance or 'Clunewic', the valley of stones was mentioned in the Domesday Book of 1086 and was at that time owned by Turstin, the Sheriff of Cornwall. Sir Henry de Kemyel between 1209 and 1214 granted the monks of St Michael's Mount a cartload of wood, the rights of pannage for their pigs and pasture for their oxen.

The sign advises that many of the family and estate records were destroyed in a fire in 1843, and that the St Aubyns initially settled in Somerset before Guy St Aubyn married an heiress from St Mabyn, near Bodmin, Cornwall. It is not clear at what point the St Aubyn family came to Clowance, but they were granted a Coat of Arms in 1545 and these arms are displayed on the side of the main house.

As with many great historical houses the impact of death duties and tax led to the estate being broken up and sold in 1919. During World War 2 the estate was used to house American servicemen and 'became a prisoner of war camp for Italians'.

Clowance House is less than three miles from the Godolphin Estate, and the families were effectively neighbours. Individuals of both the St Aubyn and Godolphin families served as member of Parliament for Cornwall over the sixteen and early seventeen-hundreds. After the Civil War ended the St Aubyn family prospered under the new regime, whereas the Godolphins' fortunes declined with their estate being seized by Parliament. The Godolphin family did regain their estate and then their fortunes really improved during the period known as the Restoration, following the return and coronation of King Charles II. The lasting family legacy was ultimately with the St Aubyn family and the purchase of St Michael's Mount. The family still live on St Michael's Mount and are involved with the local community personally and through their

St Aubyn Estates organisation. Baron St Levan of St Michael's Mount is a title that has existed for over one-hundred-and-thirty years and James and Mary St Aubyn have the title of Lord and Lady St Levan.

The causeway path leading to St Michael's Mount is located next to the Godolphin Arms on its Marazion side. This popular hotel and restaurant is owned by the St Aubyn Estate and for me it evokes a memory of the historical link between the two families.

MOUNT'S BAY

TO LIVE BY THE SEA was always an ambition of mine having grown up in one of the most inland towns of the British Isles. Residing on Mount's Bay with views out to sea has surpassed my original goal. It is fascinating to see the different colours of the sea and skies through the changing weathers and different seasons. At times the views seem to change hourly.

In the past I could always look at the causeway going to St Michael's Mount to see if the tide was in or out, but having lived here some time I can look to some distant rocks offshore and know exactly when low tide has been reached. The largest of the rocks in this particular shoal is called Little London, and this is about one-and-a-half-kilometres east of St Michael's Mount. This small formation is a single sliver of dark rock about one-hundred-and-twenty metres long. An island at high tide, it almost connects to the mainland at low tide through a necklace of smaller rocks that appear out of the water. When this necklace is completely visible then low tide has been reached. Over time I have noticed how completely different the characteristics of the rocks near the coastline at Little London are to the adjacent coastline cliffs. The coastline is a yellow sandstone and somewhat fragile, the rocks at their base and stretching out into the sea are hard granite like boulders.

Mount's Bay is named after St Michael's Mount and covers forty-two miles of coastline that stretches from the Lizard Point to Gwennap Head on the Land's End and Penwith Peninsula. The coastline between the Lizard Point and Marazion is a designated Area of Outstanding Natural Beauty (AONB) under the National Parks and Access to the Countryside Act 1949.

With the exception of three miles of coastline, Mount's Bay links the Lizard Point, the most southerly point of the British Isles with its most westerly point, Land's End. According to the English antiquarian and map maker Thomas Moule (1784 – 1851), ships leaving the English Channel dated their departure at the Lizard Point. The current lighthouse at the Lizard Point was built in 1751, with Trinity House taking on the responsibility for the lighthouse from 1771.

The Mount's Bay coastline is steep and rocky for the most part, and in places such as the Lizard Point shoal rocks go out some distance from the coastline. Over the centuries there have been numerous shipwrecks along the coast and lists of the wrecks go back to the early 1300s. On the south Cornish coastal path a large cross has been erected between Porthleven and Rinsey Cove, which has written on its base:

THIS CROSS HAS BEEN ERECTED

IN MEMORY OF THE MANY MARINERS

DROWNED ON THIS PART OF THE COAST

FROM TIME IMMEMORIAL

AND BURIED ON THE CLIFF HEREABOUT

ALSO TO COMMEMORATE

THE PASSING OF THE GRYLLS ACT OF 1808

SINCE WHEN BODIES CAST UP BY THE SEA

HAVE BEEN LAID TO REST

IN THE NEAREST CONSECRATED GROUND

ERECTED MARCH 1949

On the opposite side of the base of the cross is another sign which continues:

ALSO IN SACRED MEMORY

OF 22 PORTHLEVEN FISHERMEN

WHO LOST THEIR LIVES

IN THE FOLLOWING DISASTERS

DESIRE 1871. MIRIAM 1886

JOHANNA 1876. NILE 1893

ENERGETIC 1948

One of the larger wrecks in Mount's Bay was HMS Warspite, a Queen Elizabeth Class Battleship launched in 1913, that saw active service in both World Wars. By 1946 the Warspite had been decommissioned and was under tow from Portsmouth when on April 23, 1947, in storm force weather, the ship became detached from the tugs and ran aground on Cudden Point on Mount's Bay. It later re-floated itself at high tide, before running aground again at Prussia Cove. On April 24, 1947 the reduced crew on board were successfully rescued by a Royal National Lifeboat Institution (RNLI) lifeboat from the Penlee Lifeboat station.

The Warspite was partially scrapped before being towed the relatively short distance offshore of Marazion in 1950. Here the Warspite was beached near to St Michael's Mount, and for the next five years the Warspite was progressively cut up and scrapped. It was not until 1955 that the hull was finally lifted off the rock and this turned out to be a huge salvage operation involving the use of jet engines and compressors to finally remove the last remnants of the Warspite. Nicknamed the Grand Old Lady, the Warspite had been on active service since the Battle of Jutland in 1916 until the end of the Second World War in 1945. During the Battle of Calabria in 1940, the Warspite hit a moving enemy vessel at a range of twenty-four kilometres, making it one of the longest-range gunnery hits from a moving vessel.

On the shore at Marazion is a memorial stone to HMS Warspite, which was unveiled by Admiral Sir Charles Madden on September 25, 1992, and prayers were read out by a former crew member. A memorial using part of the ship's mast has also been erected on the headland near Prussia Cove, just a few yards off of the South Cornwall Coastal Footpath.

The coastline from the Lizard Point and around the Land's End Peninsula is renowned for shipwrecks. Over the centuries hundreds, if not thousands, of vessels have met their end due to a combination of factors, including storms, reefs, strong currents and rocky shoals that lurk below or close to the surface of the sea. There are listings of shipwrecks in the area and there is even a Shipwreck Treasure Museum in Charlestown harbour, which was fascinating to visit. Several significant shipwrecks in Mount's Bay are registered under the Protection of Wrecks Act 1973, and these include:

ST ANTHONY (SANTO ANTONIO) – JANUARY 15, 1527

The Santo Antonio, a Portuguese Carrack (one of the largest types of ship at that time) was wrecked during a terrible storm at Gunwalloe Bay. The ship and its valuable contents, which included copper and silver ingots, were the personal property of King John III of Portugal (1502 – 1557) and he demanded their return. The demand resulted in King Henry VIII setting up a Court of Star Chamber in Westminster. It appears some of the cargo was returned, but much had gone missing, and, as noted earlier, part of the dining room ceiling at Godolphin House was said to have been carved from wood recovered from the wreck.

The wreck itself then went missing for four-hundred-and-fifty years. Following the discovery of copper ingots an investigation was organised, and the wreck was located, which in turn led to its registration under the Protection of Wrecks Act 1973.

THE RILL COVE WRECK – BETWEEN 1616 AND 1618

Possibly a Spanish Merchant ship that was lost in Rill Cove (near Kynance Cove and a short distance from the Lizard Point). This was a well-known wreck that was carrying silver and coin. It was the subject of contemporaneous royal correspondence and documentation, as competing interests sought to benefit from the treasure on the submerged wreck. It seems that several opportunist divers may have taken part of the consignment, but the wreck location proved too difficult to salvage and the wreck itself was soon buried under sand and gravel. There the wreck remained obscured for centuries until it was discovered again in 1969. However, the amount of sand covering the wreck site prevented further exploration and it remains largely untouched. The site was registered in 1976.

THE SCHIEDAM – APRIL 4, 1684

The remains of an English transport vessel named the Schiedam, which became stranded near Jangye Ryn (Dollar Cove) Gunwalloe, after being caught in a storm. The vessel was carrying passengers, horses, stores and military equipment from Tangier to England and had previously been a vessel in the Dutch East India service. There were no records of survivors. The site was discovered in 1971 with its canons still visible, and was registered in 1982.

HMS ROYAL ANNE GALLEY NOVEMBER 10, 1721

HMS Royal Anne Galley was the last dual-oared and sail-fighting ship to be built by the British Navy. Classified as a forty-two gun fifth-rate frigate, HMS Royal Anne Galley was built in Woolwich dockyard in 1709. The ship had left the UK and was on its way to the West Indies, carrying Lord Belhaven on board, who was to be the next Governor of Barbados. Caught in a storm, the ship was attempting to return to port at Falmouth when it ran aground and was wrecked. Save for two or three survivors, the rest of the crew and passengers, nearly two hundred people, were all lost, including Lord Belhaven. The wreck was discovered in the 1990s and registered in 2006.

There was a legend of a mass burial of the deceased crew and passengers on nearby Pistil Meadow, a story that had been narrated many times over the years. The author and playwright William Wilkie Collins (1824 – 1889), who wrote 'The Moonstone' and 'The Woman in White', visited Cornwall several times. In his book 'Rambles Beyond Railways Or Notes In Cornwall Taken A – Foot (1861)' he recorded the following about the Pistil Meadow:

Some hundred years since, a transport ship, filled with troops, was wrecked on the reef off Lizard Head. Two men only were washed ashore alive. Out of the fearful number that perished, two hundred corpses were driven up on the beach below Pistol Meadow; and there they were buried by the tens and twenties together in great pits, the position of which is still revealed by the low irregular mounds that chequer the surface of the field. The place was named, in remembrance of the quantity of fire-arms – especially pistols – found about the wreck of the ill-fated ship, at low tide on the reef below the cliffs.

Pistil meadow is on land administered by the National Trust who asked the Maritime Archaeological Sea Trust (MAST) to investigate the area and to determine if the stories of graves was true. This survey was carried out by MAST between 2014 and 2016 using earth resistivity and other methods, but they found no evidence to confirm the graves.

LOE BAR WRECK, THE PRESIDENTS – FEBRUARY 1684

The Presidents wreck near Loe Bar is of a five hundred ton armed English East Indiaman built in 1672, caught in a storm on its return voyage from India to London. It was claimed to be the richest shipwreck in Cornwall and the cargo contained jewellery, diamonds, spices and other goods. A map of west Cornwall by the Dutch cartographer G Van Keulen, published in 1728, showed the Land's End and Penwith Peninsula, and the full extent of Mount's Bay to the Lizard Point. The map also identified the location where the ship Presidents was lost at Loe Bar in 1684. The spoils of the wreck were able to be retrieved at least in part and within the wreck site the guns and anchor are still visible. Most of the crew were lost and there were only two survivors. The site was located in the late 1990s and was registered in 1999.

The examples given are just a few of the more significant wrecks that have occurred in the Mount's Bay area, but tragically there were hundreds more. The stretch of sea between the Isles of Scilly and Land's End is also hazardous with isolated rocky outcrops. On March 18, 1967 the SS Torrey Canyon, a super-tanker laden with crude oil, ran aground on the seven stones reef, which is located some twenty kilometres west of Land's End. As the tanker broke up oil spilled into the sea causing an environmental disaster. Ten days later the air services bombed and napalmed the stricken vessel until it finally sunk. This bombing destroyed the hull of the ship, sending plumes of dense black smoke into the sky as the wreckage slipped into the sea. The burning of the oil was partially successful, but reports of oil washing up in the Channel Island of Guernsey gives some idea of the scale of the catastrophe. The Scilly Isles has also seen numerous wrecks and on October 21 and 22, 1707, four naval vessels were lost in quick succession as HMS Association, HMS Eagle, HMS Romney and HMS Firebrand all ran aground in what became known as the greatest maritime disaster of the age. It estimated that up to two-thousand people were lost in the tragedy, including Admiral Sir Cloudesley Shovell. A memorial is located on Porth Hellick on the Scilly Isles.

The introduction of lighthouses improved the safety of the ships significantly, and of the eight lighthouses in and around Cornwall, six are situated on Mount's Bay or near the Land's End and Penwith Peninsula.

These lighthouses are all different in character, and on the more exposed locations the construction is a testament to the ingenuity and endurance of the builders. All of the lighthouses are within sight of the Cornish coastal path in the area although you need a fair day to see The Wolf Rock Lighthouse from Land's End. With the exception of the Lizard and Godrevy Lighthouses, all of the others are to the west of the St Michael's Way footpath linking the north and south coast of Cornwall at its narrow point between Carbis Bay and Marazion. It is little wonder that travellers preferred this short land route to sailing around the peninsula.

The Wolf Rock Lighthouse is one of the most impressive lighthouses I know. Built by Trinity House and completed in 1869, the lighthouse sits on a small rocky outcrop nine miles south-west of Land's End. This outcrop of rock breaks the sea surface in calmer weather and is only two to three times bigger than the area occupied by the lighthouse. A real hazard for shipping and a lonely, remote, inhospitable part of the sea. Three lighthouse keepers would undertake fifty-six day shifts and hope that the weather would be calm enough for the crew changeover not to be delayed. The living conditions were cramped and there were only two spaces that were dedicated for the lighthouse keepers, the bedroom which consisted of circular bunks fixed to the lighthouse wall and a small kitchen/diner. The entrance door at the base of the lighthouse had metal supporting bars to reinforce its weathertightness against the stormy seas, which would crash against it in poor weather. What a lonely place that must have been in years past when the supply boat cast off and left the lighthouse keepers alone and isolated. Such was the difficulty getting lighthouse crew on and off the rock, that a helipad was built in 1972. It must have been a terrifying experience being in a storm with the bottom of the lighthouse submerged by water. And even in calmer weather, being situated in such a remote area with no immediate land in sight, it must have been lonely and stressful for the lighthouse keepers when working their shifts.

The magazine Cornwall Life, listed in their January 2020 edition the top ten coastal storm spots in Cornwall. Of the ten, four are on Mount's Bay and two are on the Land's End peninsula, which demonstrates just how bad the weather conditions can be on this part of the coastline. The Spectator Magazine of February 15, 2020, advised that the highest windspeed ever recorded in England was one-hundred-and-eighteen miles per hour at Gwennap Head, just south of Land's End. These winds would have whistled over the Wolf Rock Lighthouse just to the south-west.

The other lighthouse I often visit is part of National Trust property near Hayle. Godrevy Lighthouse is located on Godrevy rock to the east side of St Ives Bay, and it is a beautiful walk along the coast with its dunes and sandy beaches. The lighthouse was built in 1859 following the wreck of an iron screw steamer the SS Nile on November 30, 1854, where all passengers and crew were lost. The lighthouse is said to have been the inspiration for Virginia Woolf's, *To The Lighthouse*, published in 1927. Virginia Woolf had spent many childhood holidays in Cornwall near Gwithian.

Even with modern navigation equipment the coastguard is still kept active and the RNLI continuously work to save lives at sea. Tragically on December 19, 1981, the crew of the RNLI lifeboat Solomon Browne lost their lives trying to save the crew of the MV Union Star. The mini bulk carrier had lost the use of its engines in a storm and had been blown towards Boscawen Cliffs on the peninsula west of Lamorna Cove. In attempting the rescue in hurricane force winds and fifty-foot waves, the eight crew of the Solomon Browne lifeboat died along with eight people from the MV Union Star. The Penlee lifeboat station from which the

Solomon Browne launched closed in 1983, and the RNLI now operate out of the harbour in nearby Newlyn. The old Penlee station has been kept and has a memorial garden and granite marker in memory of the crew, who gave their lives in service. There is also a memorial stone in the nearby St Pol De Leon Parish Church in Paul village and an account of the rescue attempt. In 2019 Great Western Railway named one of its Penzance to London intercity trains the Solomon Browne in memory of the men from Mousehole.

Once I had visited and located the old lifeboat station, I realised that I could see its launching ramp and red doors at distance from my house across the bay, provided it was a clear day, and best when viewed with the morning light shining on it. The parish church at Paul which houses the memorial is also in sight and is about one kilometre away from the lifeboat station as the crow flies. Both buildings look out over Mount's Bay.

Much has been written about Mount's Bay in fiction and in non-fiction. Sir Arthur Conan Doyle used a small cottage near Poldhu Bay as his setting for one of his Sherlock Holmes stories. Poldhu Bay is near Mullion Cove on Mount's Bay and just about a mile to the east of Gunwalloe's Church Cove. He sets the scene:

> *From the windows of our little whitewashed house, which stood upon a grassy headland, we looked down upon the whole sinister semicircle of Mount's Bay, that old death trap of sailing vessels, with its fringe of black cliffs and surge-swept reefs on which innumerable seamen have met their end. With a northerly breeze it lies placid and sheltered, inviting the storm-tossed craft to tack into it for rest and protection. Then come the sudden swirl round of the wind, the blustering gale from the southwest, the dragging anchor, the lee shore, and the last battle in the creaming breakers. The wise mariner stands far out from that evil place.*

Guglielmo Marconi (1874 – 1937) also stayed in the area, at the Housel Bay Hotel in the early nineteen-hundreds during the establishment of Marconi station, built near the Lizard Point. In early 1901, a radio message was received at this station from a transmitter on the Isle of Wight, nearly two-hundred miles away.

Marconi also built a radio transmission station on the cliffs above nearby Polhu Cove. This was the first large radio transmitter in the world and on December 12, 1901 the station sent the first ever transatlantic message to St John's in Newfoundland. The use of radio communications enabled ship to shore communications and revolutionised vessel safety at sea. The Poldhu station remained commercially operational until 1922 and was later used for research until 1934. A large hotel was built nearby to house the Marconi workers and was named the Poldhu Hotel. Situated prominently above Poldhu Cove, the hotel was just a few hundred metres from the tall radio masts used for the lang range transmissions. Over time the hotel changed hands and the building is now used as a residential care home. This grand structure is visible from Mullion Cove through to Gunwalloe Cove on the south Cornwall coastal path. The future King George V and Queen Mary visited Poldhu and the Marconi station on July 18, 1903.

Facing out to sea by the radio masts above Poldhu Cove is a monument erected in 1937 by the Marconi Company to commemorate the achievements of the station and Guglielmo Marconi. After they had finished with the site the Marconi Company presented the land to the National Trust, with an initial six acres in 1957, and a further forty-four acres in 1960.

On a return visit to Mullion Cove I walked along the south Cornwall coastal path towards Poldhu on a hazy afternoon as the sun was dropping on the horizon. From the Carrag Luz Rock east of Polurrian, the view over Mount's Bay opens up and in the foreground is the Marconi Monument with two tall radio masts standing nearby. Immediately behind is the old Poldhu Hotel and above this, and slightly inland, is the village of Breage and its parish church tower standing out. Behind Breage is Tregonning Hill, the tallest marker on the landscape, visibly demonstrating its overview of the area, covering Mount's Bay from Mousehole to Mullion. Drifting into sight, in and out through the summer haze, was St Michael's Mount, sitting in the bay beyond the cliffs near Perranuthnoe. It was a moment to reflect on the beauty of this rugged coastline and how the ancient and the modern came together to forge the present.

THE TOWNS OF WEST MOUNT'S BAY

Living in the West Mount's Bay area is a privilege and it has been fascinating finding out more about the history and people of the place where I live. I'm indebted to friends who have shared stories, and have pointed me in the right direction on my searches, and in some cases told me where a sign was that I had been in search of for months. The following towns are all on Mount's Bay and are within sight of St Michael's Mount.

Marazion

Marazion is one of the oldest market towns in the country and in the town square there is a granite marker, which announces:

MARAZION WELCOMES YOU

MARGHAS YOW GOZ WELCUMBA

MARAZION IS ONE OF THE OLDEST TOWNS IN

THE COUNTRY. THE FIRST CHARTER OF

INCORPORATION WAS GRANTED IN 1257 BY
HENRY III AND THE SECOND IN 1595 BY
ELIZABETH I. THE NAME MARAZION, WITH MANY
VARIATIONS IN THE SPELLING, COMES FROM
THE CORNISH 'MARGHAS YOW'
– THURSDAY MARKET.

The name for the town has changed over the years and since the eleven hundreds there have been over one hundred recorded variants of the name, including Market Jew, Markayowe, Marghas Yow and Marca-iewe amongst others. Some property title deeds for Marazion still record land as within Market Jew, as do some of the older maps.

Marazion is included within the South Coast – Western Area of Outstanding Natural Beauty (AONB). It marks the western boundary of this southern designated AONB, which runs along the coastline from Marazion to the Helford River on the east side of the Lizard Peninsula.

Located directly opposite St Michael's Mount, the town of Marazion attracts a huge number of tourists each year, who then cross the causeway to the Mount at low tide. The tide on the causeway comes in quickly, and in the summer, it is a common sight to see visitors paddling or even wading across where they have been caught out for time. For those who do find themselves stranded, there is a regular boat service from the mount harbour to Marazion boat quay at high tide.

The town retains much of its old charm, with period buildings, small art and antique shops and a central triangular grass area bounded by restaurants and establishments offering accommodation. Many of the cottage names in the village hint to their previous use. These include

The Old Toll Cottage on Turnpike Hill, with its large granite post and hinge that once held a substantial gate to close the road. Other examples include Coachman's Cottage, Stables Cottage and there is also a Gull Cottage, which I thought had just picked a seaside name at random, but the seagulls really do home in on the roof ridge of that particular building. Some of the larger houses also show their previous use as The Old Manse, The Old Forge and Old Police House.

The coastal path, which goes all the way around Cornwall, traverses through the town centre as the beach to the east of the town is unpassable at high tide. From this elevated part of town there are panoramic views of Mount's Bay and St Michael's Mount.

Until 1964 Marazion had its own railway station, but this was closed in order to reduce costs, and because of its close proximity to the larger train station in Penzance. The building still remains on the west side of the town and the Great Western Railway trains pass close to the station on their way to and from Penzance. These trains link Cornwall directly to the cities of Plymouth, Bristol, Exeter, Reading and London. In the village of Long Rock, and in between Marazion station and Penzance station, is the main maintenance depot of the Great Western Railway.

Just on the western outskirts of town is Marazion Marsh. The marsh is a protected area that consists of two separate bodies of water surrounded by reeds and marshland. The area is a designated Royal Society for the Protection of Birds (RSPB) site and ornithologists visit throughout the year, taking watch from several viewing points on the coastal side. The marsh is also a designated Site of Special Scientific Interest (SSSI). The grey herons are often in view and the other birds that can be seen are little egrets, starlings and chiffchaffs. Being near the coast, the seagulls are ever present and if you are living in the area you will observe a turf war between the crows and the seagulls, who are often in aerial combat.

Even the local buzzard, a medium sized bird of prey, is often challenged by the crows and moved on.

On the east side of the marsh is the St Michael's Way footpath, which winds through the countryside and up to the village of Ludgvan. From Ludgvan this path crosses over the peninsula towards St Ives, emerging near Carbis Bay. The St Michael's Way was a land bridge for travellers arriving in the ports of St Ives, Lelant and Hayle to travel to the southern port of Marazion without having to sail around the Land's End peninsula.

The Way of St Michael is part of the Ways of St James, an extensive network of pilgrim routes in Europe. The path is on public rights of way across fields and farms and links St Michael's Mount on the south coast with the Church of St Uny, Lelant on the north coast. The section near the bird sanctuary and marsh is a treat to walk through as you are on the boundary of the reed marshes and waterways with their resident birds. Part of the path is elevated on a wooden slatted walkway as you traverse over the wet marshy ground under the canopy of the trees.

The ports of Hayle and Lelant on the north coast of Cornwall were an important transit point for pilgrims from Ireland, Wales and the northwest coast of Britain. Although in existence for centuries, the St Michael's Way was formally opened by His Excellency the Ambassador of Spain on May 7, 1994. The path is linked with the Camino de Santiago, a pilgrimage in northern Spain, and thousands of people make this walking pilgrimage every year. A certificate of accomplishment is given to those who complete the one-hundred-and-twenty-miles of the path, and the miles walked on the St Michael's Way count towards the mileage needed for pilgrims to receive their confirmation of pilgrimage on the Camino de Santiago. The signs indicating the footpath direction are also marked 'Pilgrim Route to Santiago'.

The Methodist minister John Wesley preached numerous times in Marazion. His journal dates these visits as August 20, 1773, August 29, 1781, August 24, 1782, August 24, 1785, and August 24, 1789. His first visit to the town was in 1745 and he would have passed by many times on his way to preaching engagements in nearby Penzance, Newlyn and Mousehole. His preaching attracted large congregations and Marazion had a large Methodist Church and a Wesleyan Church. These were both built more than seventy-five years after his visits, and while the Methodist Church remains, the Wesleyan Church passed into private ownership, and is now a residence.

Marazion was once the largest town on the Mount's Bay coastline and was a transit point for the shipment of tin and copper to overseas traders. The harbour on St Michael's Mount was the main location for the trading ships to come in and load with tin, copper and other ores. Why the harbour on the Mount was chosen is open to some speculation. It probably had to do with security and limiting traders' access to the mainland.

Penzance

Penzance is from the Cornish word *Pennsans*, meaning holy headland and there is a granite marker outside Penzance train station welcoming passengers in Cornish and English. The Great Western Railway terminates its most westerly services at Penzance. It is literally at the end of the line.

With the largest population of the towns on Mount's Bay, Penzance is home to the major hospital and medical facilities in the area. When travelling west on the A30, Penzance is the gateway through to the other towns and villages on the Land's end and Penwith Peninsula. As a sign of more prosperous times gone by, the pavements and road drainage channels of the main high street are cut from solid granite blocks, and in a link with Marazion the main high street is named Market Jew Street.

The history of Penzance is somewhat obscure and nearby Marazion was said to have been the larger of the two towns historically. Unlike the surrounding parishes, there is no existing parish church from the period before AD 1300 and Penzance only became a separate parish in 1871. St Mary's church is the largest of the churches in Penzance and this Grade II listed building is located near the seafront promenade. The church was opened in 1836 on the site of a former chapel dating from before 1321.

Towards the top of the main high street there is a statue of Sir Humphrey Davy, Baronet, who was born in Penzance in 1778. Humphrey Davy grew up in Penzance and in 1787 his family moved to a farm in the nearby village of Varfell. After leaving Penzance grammar school in 1793, he studied for two years in Truro, before returning to Penzance where he was indentured to a local surgeon, John Bingham Borlase, in 1795. Details of the Indenture are contained on public documents and the register of duties paid show that the indenture of Humphrey Davy commenced on February 28, 1795. John Bingham Borlase was the great nephew of Dr William Borlase (1696 – 1772), the famous antiquarian. Dr William Borlase was the brother of John Bingham's grandfather, George Borlase (1697 – 1769).

Back in Penzance, Humphrey Davy learned and practised chemistry and there is a plaque just off the main high street commemorating his birthplace and the time he worked as an apprentice in the town. He enjoyed walking and would stroll along the coast to Marazion after finishing his work to visit and have tea with an aunt. He was also a keen fisherman and would fish off Battery Rocks in Penzance, close to where the Jubilee Pool saltwater lido is now located. Multi-talented, Humphrey Davy was at times an author, poet and artist as well as chemist and pioneer in the use of electrolysis. Penlee Gallery in Penzance has several watercolours painted by Humphrey Davy and I was particularly impressed by his rendition of Loch Lomond, which was on display when I visited. He is remembered by miners for the invention of the Davy Lamp, which provided light in the mines and eliminated the dangers of gas explosions that occurred when candles and naked flames came into contact with combustible gas.

The other achievements credited to Davy were the discovery of sodium, potassium, barium, calcium, strontium, magnesium and boron. He was knighted in 1812 and made a baronet, a hereditary title bestowed by the Crown, in 1818. Due to ill health he passed away at the relatively young age of fifty in Geneva, and his assistant Michael Faraday, another brilliant scientist, continued his work. There is a memorial to Davy's parents, Robert and Grace, within Ludgvan Parish Church, which records that they were from the parish and worked a farm in nearby Varfell. Having rich soil deposits Varfell is still largely agricultural, and on the outskirts of the village is the National Dahlia Collection which displays the largest variety of dahlias I have ever seen. When I visited Ludgvan Parish Church I observed that the memorial to Davy's parents was prominently placed opposite the memorial of Dr William Borlase, who was the Rector of Ludgvan Parish Church for many years.

Penzance is surrounded by mining districts, and there was some mining taking place in the village of WherryTown, which is now part of Penzance. The entrance to the mine was located between the high tide and low tide water mark on the beach, and a wooden and stone tower was built to prevent water going into the mine shaft. In 1798 it is claimed that an American ship broke its moorings while in the bay and drifted towards the mine tower located at the seafront of Wherrytown. Apparently, the ship struck the shaft tower, causing the mine to flood and consequently putting an end to the mining operations. Whatever the actual reason, the mine did close in 1798.

Penzance has grown over the years and is a key link to the Isles of Scilly, with the RMV Scillonian III sailing daily from Penzance harbour to St Mary's.

A new helicopter service located near Penzance provides an alternate transportation service to the Isles of Scilly and started in July 2020. The previous helicopter service had closed several years ago leaving air access to the Isles of Scilly by light plane only.

Not far from the top of the main high street in Penzance is a plaque to John and Catherine Sampson, who lived near the location of what was the Old Post Office in 1850. Their son John Sampson and his wife left Penzance in 1854 and emigrated to Australia. Their grandson was Robert Menzies, who became the twelfth Prime Minister of Australia and was in office from 1939 – 1941 and 1949 – 1966. When he was sixteen Robert Menzies studied at Wesley College in Melbourne, later going on to study law. The Methodist minister John Wesley was a regular visitor to Penzance and the surrounding area. His brother Charles Wesley had also visited the town on several occasions.

Newlyn

Newlyn is built on the side of a hill that descends down to the sea front and harbour. The town has steep narrow roads going up the hills, making it difficult to navigate in heavy traffic. The glass windows in the town's houses catch the light from the morning sun making them sparkle when viewed from Mount's Bay. These reflections start as a few windows catch the sun, and then, as the sun's angle changes, large parts of the town start to light up.

The town of Newlyn is to the west of Penzance and the two towns are tentatively connected along the seafront of Mount's Bay by the urban sprawl between them. Newlyn was popular with artists from the nineteenth century onwards, and these artists grouped together to form what was known as the Newlyn School. Many of the works from the artists of the Newlyn School are on display at the Penlee House Gallery & Museum in Penzance.

For many years Newlyn was part of the parish of Paul and there was no separate parish church in Newlyn. It was not until the mid-1900s that the church of St Peter was built in the town of Newlyn and it became a separate parish. It now seems odd that this was the case, since Newlyn is by far the more populated place and Paul seems such a small, quiet village by comparison.

There is a plaque near the quayside noting that the Mayflower stopped by Newlyn in 1620 to take on water as it made its voyage from Plymouth to America with the Pilgrim Fathers. Another plaque at the Royal National Mission to Deep Sea Fishermen, near Newlyn harbour, records the epic voyage of seven men from Newlyn, who set out for Australia on a small lugger named the Mystery in 1854. The men had been discussing the poor prospects of Cornish mining and fishing, and were speculating that they could make a fortune gold mining in Australia. This idea took hold and Richard Nichol, who was the captain of the lugger Mystery, agreed to take them. The voyage took just short of four months and covered nearly twelve thousand nautical miles. After landing in Melbourne the men sold the Mystery for one-hundred-and-fifty-pounds and five of the seven men returned home. Philip Mathews and Lewis Lewis decided to stay on in Australia, and although they had discussed going into gold mining it seems that neither did. Lewis Lewis worked as a shepherd and died in 1866, eleven years after his arrival. Philip Mathews worked as a surveyor in Melbourne and passed away in 1896. In 2008, one hundred and fifty-four years after Mystery sailed out of Newlyn for the last time, a repeat voyage was made from Newlyn to Melbourne in a replica ship named the Spirit of Mystery.

Newlyn retains a large-scale fishing industry to this day and the UK Sea Fisheries Statistic report of 2017 had Newlyn as the second largest fishing industry in England and Wales. Around the harbour there are numerous shops selling the freshly caught produce and until recently Newlyn celebrated an annual fish festival on the north quayside.

Mousehole

Mousehole was traditionally a fishing village and has a picturesque harbour at its centre. Within the harbour small boats are tied up over a small sandy shore, which is prominent at low tide. Rising up from the harbour the village is built up the side of a hill, and access to the sea front by vehicle is restricted through two steep and narrow roads, which operate as part of a one-way system. The southern part of the Cornish coastal path passes through Mousehole and it is a popular destination for tourists who visit the small shops and cosy cafes along the sea front. Mousehole is included within the Penwith Area of Outstanding Natural Beauty (AONB) and this area stretches from Mousehole all around the south, west and north of the peninsula to St Ives.

As with Newlyn, Mousehole was part of the parish of Paul, which is located at the top of the steep road out of the village. The residents of Mousehole would have had a challenging climb from the harbour to attend the services at the Parish Church in Paul.

Writing in his 1728 work *A Topographical and Historical Description of Cornwall*, John Norden recorded variants of the town's name as

Mowshole and Meddeshole and noted that in Cornish it was called Port-ernis or Port-inis. He went on to add that near Mousehole, 'certain tynners in their minerals founde armour, Spear heads, Swords, Battle axes, and such like of Copper, wrapte up in lynnen clothes, the weapons not much decayed'.

Between Mousehole and Newlyn is Penlee Quarry, also known as Gwavas Quarry. Dating from the nineteenth century the quarry was mined for copper and zinc, but in more recent times the quarry was used for the extraction of aggregate and stone. The scarred face of the hill on the perimeter of the quarry is visible from Mount's Bay and the surrounding towns. Within the quarry area there is a large lake, which is only visible from overhead. The quarry used a narrow-gauge railway system to bring the aggregate along the coast to Newlyn, where it was shipped out. The railway was in use up until 1973 and the railway engine car was located in Newlyn Harbour. The quarry finally closed production in 1994 and since then there has been plans to transform the lake and surrounding quarry into a marina and housing development.

MOUNT'S BAY PAST AND PRESENT

Past

Driving across the Land's End and Penwith Peninsula on the roads that criss-cross from north to south, and west to east, it is surprising how far inland you can be, but still catch a distant glimpse of Mount's Bay and St Michael's Mount. From Sancreed Beacon in the west of the peninsula and Trencrom in the north, and other high points in between, there are sight lines that stretch for miles down to the west side of Mount's Bay. I find the bay is a centre of interest for the area, and over time it has become the most populous part of the peninsula with the towns of

Newlyn, Penzance and Marazion dominating in terms of size and population. The inland towns on the Land's End and Penwith Peninsula were once sizeable enough to support the construction and maintenance of parish churches, and brought the population close to the mines, which had been active since ancient times. It seemed to me that the relatively recent migration from the towns on the peninsula to the coast was linked to the decline of the mining industry, and the improved sea and rail transport links from the larger population centres. In the past the coast was considered vulnerable to attack, from all sorts of different sources including pirates, slavers, raiders or foreign powers. This was not only true for Cornwall, it was the same for other parts of the United Kingdom, and that is why so much was spent on coastal defences across time. Given the natural cliff line around the Land's End and Penwith Peninsula, it made complete sense to live above the sea and be able to look out across Mount's Bay.

Mining in Cornwall could have started as early as 2,500 BC and evidence at the Iron Age settlement of Chysauster, which is also within sight of Mount's Bay, indicates that they were smelting tin ore over two thousand years ago. Exactly when mining for tin and copper started is not known, but it is known that it was a well-established during the Iron Age, and most likely earlier started in the Bronze Age.

The use of bronze began around 3,000 BC and produced a revolution in the use of metal up to that point. The discovery of this versatile metal, which was an alloy of tin and copper, heralded the period that became known as the Bronze Age.

Bronze could be used both functionally and decoratively, and during this era, weapons such as spears, shields and swords were forged from bronze, giving those civilisations who had access to this metal a decisive advantage over those that did not. Bronze was also used in the production of domestic goods such as cups, basins and bowls and was able to be worked intricately into beautiful jewellery. The Bronze Age in turn preceded the Iron Age.

The Egyptians were the first to use bronze on a large scale during the period of the pharaohs, and they became one of the dominant civilizations at that time. As with other Pharaohs, the tomb of King Tutankhamun held bronze artefacts amongst its many treasures. Egypt may have had some small deposits of tin and copper ore, but it was not sufficient to meet their growing domestic demand. As other nations and civilisations also started to use bronze, the requirement for tin and copper increased and new sources of supply were needed. The Phoenicians played a key role in meeting this demand as they were a trading nation and renowned seafarers who sailed around the Mediterranean and beyond. It is known that their voyages took them out of the Mediterranean, south to Africa and north along the Iberian Peninsula. From the top of the Iberian Peninsula a voyage north-west would have brought them to Western Brittany in France and a further voyage north would bring them to Britain.

Now part of modern-day Lebanon, the Phoenician coastal ports of Sidon and Tyre were major trading cities, which distributed the copper and tin ingots brought in by their ships. The Bible mentions the use of bronze one-hundred-and-thirty-eight times, and from the accounts of King Solomon's building of the temple in Jerusalem, bronze was extensively used in a wide range of forms, from structural supports to utensils and decoration. In response to King Solomon's request for skilled help with the building of the temple, King Hiram of Tyre sent Huram-Abi, and described him *as a man of great skill, trained to work in gold and silver, bronze and iron, stone and wood.*

Naturally secretive about the source of their tin and copper, the Phoenicians referred to one of their mining locations as the Cassiterides, meaning islands of tin. The exact location of these islands is unknown other than they were beyond the Mediterranean and in Western Europe. It is possible, but by no means proven, that the islands of tin could have referred to the Isles of Scilly, and even Cornwall may have been considered an island with its deep inlets at Falmouth Bay and the river Tamar at Plymouth. A quote from Herodotus the Greek Historian (485 BC – 425 BC) confirmed that he had heard of the Cassiterides, but was not aware of their location.

Dr William Borlase, in his 'Observations on the antiquities historical and monumental, of the county of Cornwall' speculates that the Phoenician word Baratanac, meaning land of tin, could have been used to describe the location of the Phoenecian tin source. This word Baratanac in turn may have been the basis for the Romans using the term Britannia. His work also notes:

> But the principal inducement for the Phoenicians to frequent our coasts was the Tin, a metal far transcending both the beauty and the use of Lead: this Metal was anciently also found in Lusitania, and Gallaecia, but in too small quantities to satisfy the expectations of so many cities, and countries, as were desirous to have it; the Phoenicians therefore having discover'd abundance of Tin in some small British islands carry'd on so considerable a trade here that from these little islands only, among which they probably reckon'd the West of Cornwall, . . . they were enabled to supply the greatest part of the world with this useful Metal: all the cities and nations of the Mediterranean had their Tin chiefly from the Phoenicians, and they from the islands of Britain . . .

William Borlase further speculates that the Cassiterides, Islands of Tin, did in fact refer to the Isles of Scilly (or Sylleh) and West Cornwall. He went on:

> *From these islands the Phoenicians had their treasures of Tin, and were exceeding jealous of their trade, and therefore so private, and industrious to conceal it from others, that a Phoenician vessel thinking itself pursued by a Roman, chose to run upon a shoal and suffer shipwreck, rather than discover the least track, or path, by which another nation might come in for the least share of so beneficial a commerce.*

Given the Phoenicians' desire to keep their commercial ventures secret, it is perhaps understandable why there are no historical maps showing the Cassiterides or indicating their trading ports north of Spain.

Diodorus Siculas was a Greek traveller and historian, who wrote about a number of locations during the period 60 BC – 30 BC, including Britain around the time of the Roman invasion. The following is from his account of Britain in his writings entitled *Library of Histories*. Book V Chapter 22 is translated to English as follows:

> *Concerning their institutions, and other things peculiar to the island, we shall speak specially when we come to the expedition of Caesar into Britain. At this time we shall treat of the tin which is dug from the ground. Those who dwell near Belerium, one of the headlands of Britain, are especially fond of strangers, and on account of their trade with the merchants they have a more civilized manner of living. They collect the tin after the earth has been skilfully forced to yield it. Although the land is stony, it has certain veins of earth from which they melt and purify the metal which has been extracted. After making this into bars they carry it to a certain island near Britain called Ictis. For although*

the place between is for the most part covered with water, yet in the middle there is dry ground, and over this they carry a great amount of tin in wagons . . . Thence the merchants carry into Gaul the tin which they have bought from the inhabitants. And after a journey of thirty days on foot through Gaul, they convey their packs carried by horses to the mouths of the Rhone River.

There is common agreement that Belerium is the Land's End and Penwith Peninsula, and it is speculated that Ictis was St Michael's Mount. The description of an island that can be accessed by dry ground, as St Michael's Mount can be at low tide, seems to fit with no other geographical alternative presenting itself. From this account we can see that the Cornish were trading internationally, and had been for some time with supply and trading routes well established. At the time this passage was written, the Phoenician civilisation was on the wane, having peaked in its powers between 1,200 and 800 BC. The Persians under King Cyrus invaded Phoenicia in 539 BC, and Alexander the Great took Tyre in 332 BC. Since trade for Cornish tin and copper was well established in Cornwall before the Roman invasion, it opens the possibility that Greek or Roman traders were the merchants referred to by Diodorus Siculas. However, that does not rule out earlier trading with the Phoenicians.

I found these historical records fascinating as it opened up the possibility that Cornwall had been internationally trading tin and copper for thousands of years. In turn it would mean that Mount's Bay would been visited by these overseas traders as they docked and loaded these valuable metals for export. The bountiful supply of minerals and ores within Cornwall's unique geology set it apart as one of the great historical exporters of these valuable commodities.

It's incredible to think that the Phoenicians and other trading nations may have been sailing into Mount's Bay since before 400 BC after they had located one of the world's greatest hordes of minerals and metal ore.

Invasion

The towns and villages on Mount's Bay have been subject to attack and invasion over the years. One of the most significant attacks occurred in 1595 during the Anglo Spanish war. This protracted and undeclared war between Spain and England lasted from 1585 to 1604. During this period there were several key engagements with the Spanish Armada. The first was in 1588 when the Armada sailed into the English Channel and were sighted off the Lizard Point. Warning beacons were set alight up the coast and the Armada was met by English ships that sailed out of Plymouth. A year later, in 1589, an expedition led by Sir Francis Drake and Sir John Norreys sailed to northern Spain with the intention of attacking the Spanish Armada while it was being refitted in Santander, San Sebastian and Corunna. This mission had only limited success and Drake and Norreys returned to Plymouth. The second Spanish Armada was later in 1596 and this failed as a result of bad weather and a lack of proper preparations; in fact, the Armada did not make it into the English Channel. A third Spanish Armada sailed in 1597 and the weather again intervened as a tremendous storm scattered the Armada. Many ships were lost from this third Armada and there were Spanish shipwrecks at the Lizard point and on the Isles of Scilly. During the storm of 1597, Sir Walter Raleigh, on board HMS Warspite, was swept around the Cornish peninsula and sheltered in St Ives harbour to make repairs.

It was on August 2, 1595, some seven years after the first Spanish Armada and a year before the second Spanish Armada, that four Spanish galleys commanded by Carlos de Amesquita anchored off Mousehole and sent an invasion force into the harbour town. A force of four hundred men landed near to the entrance of Mousehole harbour and the town was then bombarded by the Spanish galleys. The house that Squire Jenkyn Keigwin lived in remains, and a plaque on the wall narrates that he perished defending his house in the encounter with the invaders. From the harbour Spanish troops ascended the hill to the town of Paul and set fire to the church of St Pol de Leon, causing extensive damage. The next day, August 3, 1595, the Spanish ships moved further into Mount's Bay and attacked Newlyn. On land, and without any meaningful resistance, the Spanish armed forces moved into Newlyn and then on to Penzance. A Militia force under Sir Francis Godolphin (1540 – 1608) met the Spanish soldiers and an engagement followed where the militia were scattered, some taking refuge in St Michael's Mount. Penzance was then bombarded by the galleys and it is estimated that four hundred houses were destroyed during the attack. St Mary's church was spared as the Spanish were told it had once heard Mass. The Spanish continued their looting and burning and finally left Mount's Bay on August 4, 1595.

The following year, 1596, the Spanish made landfall in Cornwall and attacked Cawsand near the Devon border.

In 1728, John Norden carried out a *Topographical and Historical Description of Cornwall* and noted of Penzance that, 'It is a market towne, but of late verie much defaced, being also burned by the Spaniardes in 1595.' Clearly the damage done was still visible nearly one hundred and fifty years later.

There had been tension between England and Spain since the early reign of King Henry VIII, who had married and then separated from Catherine of Aragon. King Henry VIII had established the Church of England, and at that same time separated from Rome and the authority of the Pope. Since Spain was a Catholic Country this set England at enmity with the Spanish. This was not the only foreign policy issue; the French sent an invasion fleet in July 1545, and King Henry VIII lost his flagship, the Mary Rose, in the Solent. Some eighteen months later King Henry VIII died, and the crown passed to his daughter Elizabeth. It was during Queen Elizabeth I's rule that the Anglo Spanish war began.

There was also an earlier incursion in 1513, when a French frigate sailed in to Mount's Bay and the crew plundered Marazion, setting fire to buildings in the town. This event is not well documented and may tie up with another account of the guns on St Michael's Mount firing on a French frigate.

Another incident that happened on the night of September 29, 1760, was initially thought to have been an invasion or a raid. A barbary corsair, thinking itself somewhere off the Spanish coast, had run ashore near Newlyn, and as the new day dawned the barbary pirates were found armed and ready to fight. The good people of Penzance and Newlyn were naturally nervous about this incursion, not least because of the reputation barbary pirates had for raiding and kidnapping people for the slave trade. Also, the country was in the middle of the Seven Years war (1756 – 1763) with French and Spanish alliances, and the arrival of this band of pirates may well have been a prelude to something bigger. As a volunteer force was pulled together, the pirates were rounded up and contained. The story emerged that the captain of the barbary corsair had miscalculated the ship's position, and with no idea where he was, had run aground in the darkness. As the ship was no longer sea-worthy, a man of war picked the pirates up and brought them back to their base in North Africa.

Tornado, Tsunami and Earthquake

On Wednesday August 27, 1760, there were reports of a waterspout that formed in the sea near Mousehole an hour before sunset. Described by eyewitnesses as about twenty yards in diameter at the bottom and broader as it reached up to the clouds, it had all the hallmarks of what we would know as a modern-day tornado, and it made a noise like thunder. This waterspout travelled across Mount's Bay, making landfall between Marazion and Penzance. One witness described it as having a strong sulphurous smell, and as it came on to the shore it dragged sand and pebbles as it travelled along. It then headed inland at four-to-five miles an hour, wreaking destruction in its path. An hour after sunset it passed near to Cambourne and was seen taking up a farmer's large haystack and eighteen sacks of corn and scattering them around the countryside, before passing out to sea. This was from an account written in John Wesley's journal.

An earthquake occurred off the coast of Portugal mid-morning on November 1, 1755, which devastated the city of Lisbon. The earthquake also triggered a huge tsunami that travelled from its epicentre in all directions. The tsunami reached Mount's Bay within hours and continued up the southern English coastline. Reports within the bay noted that the tsunami came in three waves, with the sea receding and then rising again quickly. The sea level in Mount's Bay rose eight feet in Newlyn and ten feet in Penzance. This in turn produced severe flooding to the lower parts of the coastline from Newlyn to Marazion. There are no detailed records of lives lost and damage to property, but given the size of the tsunami it must have had a devastating impact in the Mount's Bay area.

While visiting St Agnes, Cornwall on Saturday, September 3, 1757, John Wesley was told of an earthquake that had occurred on Friday, July

15, less than seven weeks earlier. He noted in his journal, 'There was first a rumbling noise under the ground, hoarser and deeper than common thunder. Then followed a trembling of the earth, which afterward waved once or twice to and fro so violently that one said he was obliged to take a back-step, or he should have fallen down; and another that the wall against which he was leaning seemed to be shrinking from him.'

The Royal Society have an abstract attributed to Dr William Borlase which states, 'On Friday the 15th of July, 1757 a violent shock of an earthquake was felt in western parts of Cornwall. The thermometer had been higher than usual and the weather hot, or calm, or both, for eight days before; wind east and north-east. On the 14th in the morning, the wind shifting to the south-west, the weather calm and hazy, there was a shower.'

Four days later after he was in St Agnes, John Wesley noted in his journal (Cambourne – Wednesday, September 7, 1757) that he witnessed the effects of a burning wind that had passed through the area on August 28. He noted that, 'It not only scorched all the leaves of the trees, so as to bring mid-winter upon them in two hours, but burned up all the leaves of the potatoes and cabbage, and every green thing that it touched.' This hot wind followed on six weeks after the surprise earthquake, and may, in some way, have been linked.

Present

Mount's Bay is active for both industry and leisure purposes. Between Long Rock and Marazion wind conditions on the bay make it an ideal location for kite and wind surfing. Whenever a storm is coming or has just passed, it is usual to see the coast between St Michael's Mount and Long Rock packed with these wind and kite surfers. It seems that the windier the better for these adventurers who can be seen leaping from wave to wave or taking off into the air for extended periods. In August 2019 the Mount's Bay Sailing Club hosted the Enterprise and Osprey National Championship for the tenth time. Racing for both classes of boats is scheduled over four consecutive days and the race circuit is set each day based on the wind strength and direction. The racecourse is marked out by large inflatable buoys, towed into final position by race officials. In 2019 I was fortunate to be included on one of the course marker positions and marked the furthest westerly point of the course. The extremities of the course are only finalized by the race committee just before the start of each race, and the race committee constantly monitor wind strength and direction before setting the final GPS locations for the buoys. There are several races for each class depending on weather conditions and it was very exciting watching the racers tack and jibe to the course marker and then turn. We were just ten metres off the buoy and had a close-up view of the frantic action involved in a racing turn. Some racers mistimed their turns and angles, which resulted in capsizing for several of the vessels. For those who got it right they were able to catch the wind behind them, open up their spinnaker sail and accelerate downwind to the next marker.

Fishing on a small scale still takes place within the sheltered part of Mount's Bay, although the commercial fishing vessels from Newlyn harbour travel much further out to sea to make their fishing viable.

Living near Mount's Bay for parts of the year, it seems there is always a visiting ship passing through, and in the distance cruise ships pass across the horizon as they journey from one destination to another. I often find myself looking out to sea and scanning across the bay for ships near and far. Some vessels stay for weeks and as I write this passage, HMS Westminster, a type 23 frigate, has been anchored up close to St Michael's Mount for two days. When a ship is in the bay for some time, you can see them day and night, with their lights on in the darkness. Sometimes I watch the ships sail away and as they disappear on the horizon I think of what adventures await them in their next journey. Other ships come and go and with modern technology, a marina navigation app will quickly tell you what that ship is in the area and where it came from. It is fascinating thinking about all these journeys criss-crossing Mount's Bay as crew and passengers journey past. In 2018 HMS Queen Elizabeth, the latest aircraft carrier commissioned by the British Navy, conducted part of its sea trials while anchored in Mount's Bay for a week. It was impressive to see the largest vessel ever built for the Navy and the helicopters flying in and out. The scene is occasionally highlighted by fighter jets screaming out over the bay from their base at the nearby Royal Naval Air Station (RNAS) Culdrose, or a search and rescue helicopter practising manoeuvres in the bay.

The larger marine traffic in Mount's Bay are mostly tankers or supply vessels anchored between commissions and waiting for their next assignment. In 2018 the BOKA Vanguard, the world's largest semi-submersible heavy lift ship, was anchored in Mount's Bay for two weeks. The ship is capable of lifting cargoes up to one hundred and ten thousand tonnes and lifted the cruise ship Carnival Vista out of the water at sea to bring it for dry dock repairs.

CHANNELS IN THE SEA

When the sea around the St Michael's Mount area of Mount's Bay is peaceful, a mosaic of contrasting colours often appears on its surface. I was not sure what caused this effect, but referred to the contrast as channels, as they seemed to wind their way through a much larger area. Over time, it became apparent that the effect happened more in the summer months than winter, and probably had more to do with sea temperature and the way the sunlight fell upon the water. It was a common occurrence, almost daily in good summer weather, but nobody ever seemed to notice or comment upon it.

Free the soft light at twilight falls,
illuminating the channels in the sea.
The contrast of deep and shallow waters,
or rip tides running free?

Flat water against ripples late in the day,
their paths a watery maze.
Casting their shadow across the bay,
accentuated in the evening haze.

Like cloud trails in the sky,
from a jet plane flying by.
Colour contrasted light and fair,
as the sun rises, they are still there.

LIGHT

When the morning sun rises from the east, it casts its light on what I believe is the best view of St Michael's Mount. As with a beautiful sunset, there is that short period where the light is just perfect, and this is equally true of the morning light. Once the dawn sun has cleared the horizon over the hills between Perranuthnoe and Marazion it unleashes its light onto St Michael's Mount. And there, for a few minutes, the light seems perfect and the subject matter framed beautifully in its spotlight.

As the early morning sun continues its path, the harbour town of Newlyn is also highlighted in its direct sunlight, causing the windows to sparkle. The effect does not last for long but can be seen anywhere from Marazion and the St Michael's Bay area.

In the evening the reverse happens as the sun sets in the west, it is the opposite side of St Michael's Mount that catches the warm golden light, and the eastern side, so beautifully lit in the morning, is silhouetted against the sunset. For me, these are the best parts – the early morning light and the promise of a new day, and later a beautiful sunset across the bay.

The castle on the mount shone
in the dawn light of a new day.
The walls bleached white,
as the sun's morning light touched the bay.

The house on the cliff basked
in the warm glow of the setting sun.
The surfaces bronzed in the sun's golden rays,
announcing that the day had been run.

The windows in the houses
caught the sun's mid-morning light.
They sparkled and twinkled like jewels in a crown
as radiant light bathed the harbour town.

RINSEY COVE

A memory stirs from long ago,
Far back to an early childhood.
Of country lanes and a walk across the cliffs,
Descending down a steep rocky path,
to a hidden cove,
nearly half a century past.

I could still recall,
the sandy beaches,
that were hidden at high tide.
We went there once,
and then no more.
But the distant memory remained,
until at last,
I found it again.

Rinsey Cove is located between Praa Sands and Porthleven on the south-west Cornish Coast, and is just below Tregonning Hill. It is a significant site of geological interest and the craggy multi-coloured granite cliffs that drop down to the crashing sea form a dramatic backdrop to the cove. I had a distant memory from one of our family holidays long ago of visiting a sandy cove that was cut off at high tide. The walk down the steep footpath to the cove and the clambering down the cliff just above the sandy floor left a lasting impression with me. The beach was unspoilt yellow sand and at the bottom of the cliffs were all sorts of sandy pools filled with sea water, trapped as the tide had gone out. It was the perfect location, and had it not been for the tide cutting off the cove twice a day, we might have spent more time there and less time at Gunwalloe beach, further along the coast.

For many years the location of the visit was lost, and it was only recently that I revisited the area and the memory returned.

The engine house of Wheal Prosper is sited prominently above the cliffs at Rinsey Cove looking out to sea. This was an active mine for six years only between 1860 to 1866 and was mined for tin and copper. The engine house and chimney stack stand out as a marker above the cliff and the building seems precariously close to the edge. Rinsey Cove is on the outer part of the Tregonning and Godolphin mining district, and the cliff face gives us a glimpse into the varied rock strata that formed in this area. I thought to myself what a contrast it would have been, emerging from that deep dark mine into the sunshine and panoramic views across the sea. Just a little further east along the coastline is the Wheal Trewavas mine with its engine houses perched precariously on the side of the cliffs. These spectacular mine buildings are just off the coastal path and located east of Trewavas Head and Rinsey Cove. The Wheal Trewavas mine was in operation between 1834 and 1846, and predates the Wheal Prosper mine.

The sandy beach is accessible at low tide from a cliff path that runs from the Cornish Coastal Footpath above the cliffs. The path is steep and rocky in places and the section just above the beach involves climbing down the sloping cliff face. This does not stop families with children getting down onto the beach and enjoying the rock pools and waves.

In World War Two Rinsey Bay was the site of a lookout station using radar to check on activity in the bay. The remains of the reinforced concrete structure is still visible although it is now somewhat overgrown with vegetation. The structure is just a few yards off Cornwall's coastal path, which passes above the cliff tops.

There was a Rinsey Rinsey Godolphin who comes up on a genealogical search. Perhaps there is an historical link between the village of Rinsey and the Godolphins, whose estate was just a few miles away?

GUNWALLOE

When we stayed at Tregonning Hill House our regular day trip was to Gunwalloe. From a combination of memory and a love of the seascape in this bay I always enjoy visiting. Gunwalloe is to the south of Helston and the Culdrose Royal Naval Air Station. The roads to the beach twist and turn through narrow lanes as you sweep downhill, and around a final corner the bay opens up and there it is, the farm, the entrance to the beach and the cliffs rising upwards in the distance. The village and the beach are both called Gunwalloe, but there is a small land separation between the two. There are two beach areas, the larger sandy bay is called Church Cove and this sits below the Mullion Golf Course on the east side of St Winwaloe Church, the other beach is in Dollar Cove which is less sandy and has an altogether more fissured granite like look about it. The area has been used for filming and features in the 2017 BBC Poldark series.

The National Trust has been connected with Gunwalloe for many years and recently purchased Winnianton Farm, which was a working farm until a few years ago. The Winnianton farmhouse is a Grade II listed building and dates back to the 1840s.

Winnianton was once the site of a Saxon Manor house and is mentioned in the Domesday Book for Cornwall. In 1086 Winnianton was referred to as the Hundred of Winnianton and encompassed thirty-four separate locations, including Rinsey and Helston. Winnianton had been the property of the Anglo-Saxon King Harrold, but this changed following the battle of Hastings in 1066 and the Norman Conquest. By 1086 the Tenant in Chief was named as King William. Gunwalloe is within Cornwall's designated AONB and the nearby Rose Cottage is a grade II listed building.

Jangye-ryn, otherwise known as Dollar Cove, was the scene of a shipwreck in 1669 when the San Salvador ran aground and broke up.

According to the National Trust, silver dollar pieces washed ashore from the wreck and this presumably gave rise to the name Dollar Cove.

Between Dollar Cove and Church Cove is St Winwaloe Church of the Storms. The church dates from the thirteenth century and is the only church in Cornwall that is built on a beach. The church is partly built into the side of headland that separates the two coves and this promontory is called Castle Mound. The location has all the qualities of a promontory fort, protected on three sides by cliffs and the sea, and reachable only by a steep uphill approach that could easily be defended. The name Castle Mound gives an indication of how this site was used in the past.

Dedicated to St Winwaloe (alternate Winnoc – Twennocus) this church is linked with the Parish Church in Towednack on the Land's End and Penwith Peninsula. The church of St Wynwallow's in Landewednack (eleven kilometres south-east of Gunwalloe and near the Lizard Peninsula) and a church in Landevennec, Brittany are also dedicated to St Winwaloe. The church tower is believed to date back to the thirteenth century with the chapel being of fourteenth and fifteenth century construction. As with other churches in Cornwall, there is a copy of a letter of thanks from King Charles I, written in 1643.

LOE POOL

Loe Pool is located south of Helston, between the harbour town of Pothleven and Gunwalloe, and is separated from Mount's Bay by a large sandbar. Also known as The Loe, it is part of the Penrose Estate, now administered by the National Trust. As with most of the coastline on this part of Mount's Bay, it is within Cornwall's AONB. The walks around the estate and Loe Pool border onto woodland, and little tributaries from the pool seep into the surrounding lowland and form tiny streams in the green valleys between the tree lines.

Penrose House and the Penrose Estate which stretches along the south coastline to Gunwalloe was given to the National Trust in 1974 by Lt. Cdr J. P Rogers. The Rogers family had owned the estate for many generations, purchasing the property from the Penrose family in 1771.

Loe Pool is a hidden gem on the south coast with its blue waters hedged in by woodland and bridleways. It is Cornwall's largest freshwater lake and the river Cober exits at this point, filling the pool with freshwater. The beginning of the river Cober is on the nine maidens down near Crowan Beacon (Crowan being the location of Clowance House, ancestral home of the St Aubyn family). The small boating lake to the south of Helston, near the old cattle market, is part of the river Cober and less than one mile to the north of Loe Pool. I remember the old cattle market when it was active, and attending a cattle auction while we were on holiday. The livestock were held in separate pens before being displayed in the auction ring as the bidding took place. The frantic activity of the auction and the farmyard smell were two memories that stand out for me. I don't know when the market closed, but I would have thought it would have been in the early to mid-seventies. A new building called 'The Old Cattle Market' now stands on the site and hosts markets, fairs and community events. It was close to this area that John Wesley would preach in the St Johns district when he visited Helston. On the hill above The Old Cattle Market is St Michael's Church, which was built between 1751 and 1761 with funds from the Earl of Godolphin.

From the boating lake I have walked several of the trails down to Loe Pool following the river Cober as it winds its way through fern covered banks and lush woodland. It is a lovely walk, full of points of interest, and then, through the trees, you suddenly catch a glimpse of Loe Pool on its southern side. Walking to the west of Loe Pool I can see the expanse of water, which is nearly always calm and flat, hemmed in on all sides. Heading further south the trail passes through to the coast above Loe Pool, and has some of the best views, especially above the sandbar itself. I always enjoy the contrast in colour and texture between the sea and Loe Pool, and at this particular junction there is a picturesque old gate house that looks over both. Sitting prominently above the sea, this gate house has been used as a filming location on numerous occasions, and has a twin gatehouse on the Helston side of Loe Pool.

An abandoned lead, tin and silver mine named Wheal Pool is on the edge of Loe marsh just north of Loe Pool. The mine is said to have been active from the 1600s and was also active in the late 1700s and early 1800s. Remnants of the granite engine house and stack are close to one of the bridleways on the approach to Loe Pool from Helston, and are perched on the side of a steep bank, which runs down to the woodland valley and river below. Water from the Loe Pool was a factor in the underground workings of the mine and in the late seventeen-hundreds the pool was partially drained into the sea to reduce the water levels. Like many mines of this time it went into and out of production, sensitive to both the prevailing rates for ore and the cost of extraction.

The National Trust, who look after Loe Pool and much of the surrounding countryside, have installed water treatment facilities to prevent the build-up of phosphorous in the water and keep the condition stable for wildlife. The whole area is in remarkably good shape and kept pristine for the enjoyment of walkers and sightseers.

On January 23, 1796, an unidentified troopship was wrecked in a heavy storm near Loe Bar. The ship was transporting an estimated six hundred officers and troops of the 26th Regiment of Dragoons. All hands were lost in the storm together with the horses that the ship was carrying. This is just one of several shipwrecks that have come aground on the Loe Bar.

THE ANCIENT SITES

W HEN I DECIDED TO WRITE this book, I had no idea that I would be covering a period so far back in history. My visit to Castle Pencair on Tregonning Hill and the remains of a Celtic settlement, had me thinking about other locations in West Cornwall that might have had ancient sites. The answer, as it turned out, was overwhelming and quite literally caused me to see this area of Cornwall from a completely new perspective. And now that I know what is out there it amazes me that I never really took notice before, or that the ancient monuments were so close at hand, literally everywhere you travel. I don't know how many times I have driven past the West Cornish Carns (Hills) and been oblivious to the fact I was just a few hundred metres from an ancient monument that was thousands of years old. Within the north region of the Land's End and Penwith Peninsula, between St Just and Zennor, many of the major stone monuments and barrows are located in a band that extends some five miles, and is just a few miles from the north coast.

The Land's End and Penwith Peninsula is surrounded by the sea on its North, West and Southern extremities and has a short land bridge to the rest of Cornwall on its east side. This land bridge is narrow and runs between Hayle estuary on the north coast and Marazion on the south coast. It is across this land bridge that the St Michael's Way footpath winds its way between the two coastlines.

Under the Ancient Monuments Protection Act of 1882, there are over fifteen-hundred scheduled monuments in Cornwall. On the Land's End and Penwith Peninsula there are two-hundred-and-twenty-six scheduled monuments that range from ancient settlements, to stone circles, stone crosses, standing stones, quoits (man-made stone features with vertical stones supporting a large stone slab), wells, remains of castle forts, and in more modern times, the granite shells of some mines have been included in the list. Not everything that is ancient is listed and not everything listed is ancient.

These ancient monuments give us an insight into how the people of this land lived and worked on the peninsula. When looking at ancient monuments it is helpful to give the age context when referring to periods in time:

The Stone Age is taken as predating 2,500 BC.
The Bronze Age is taken as 2500 BC – 800 BC.
The Iron Age is taken as 800 BC – AD 100.
And the Middle Ages is taken as AD 500 – AD 1,500.

Two thousand years ago the people of Cornwall and Devon were known as the Dumnonii tribe and this tribe inhabited an area known as Dumnonia. It is a large area of the British Isles stretching over one-hundred-and-twenty miles from east to west, with coastline on its north, south and western borders. Despite being one tribe, it would seem that the tribe was factional with sub-groups living in different locations within the overall territory.

West Cornwall and the Land's End and Penwith Peninsula has its two-hundred-and-twenty-six scheduled sites, contained in an area of just over one hundred square kilometres, or over two sites for each square kilometre as an average. That is an incredible number given the often-windswept conditions and inhospitable living conditions on this granite outcrop. The age of these sites vary considerably, and some are believed to be more than four thousand years old. In looking at the sites, I found they naturally sub divided into four main headings:

Promontory Forts – Defensive positions located on the coast and often with three of their four flanks protected by the sea and cliffs.

Hill Forts – Defensive positions built at height with fortifications.

Ancient Villages – located on the hills although not always on the summit.

Monuments – These are a selection of Quoits (stone slabs supported by stone supports), Standing Stones and Stone Circles.

I was immediately struck by how many Promontory Forts and Hill Forts there were on the Land's End and Penwith Peninsula, and decided to have a map commissioned to show them all. To give an idea of scale on the head of the peninsula, the distance between Bosigran Castle on the north coast and Treryn Dinas on the South coast is just fifteen kilometres and the distance between Lescudjack on the east side of the peninsula to Cape Cornwall on the west coast is just over twelve kilometres. In and around this relatively small area are twelve forts/castes, sixteen if we include Trencrom, Castle Pencair, Carnsew near Hayle and St Michael's Mount.

The locations of the promontory and hill forts when plotted to one map show how well defended West Cornwall was. Each of these defence sites required a huge effort to construct, particularly the hill forts where boulders and rocks used on the perimeter defences required transporting and lifting into place. The number of the forts in this location is deserving of the name 'Fortress West Cornwall'.

These fortresses were actively used in the Iron Age and several date back to an earlier point in history. They remained in use into the early centuries AD, but were gradually abandoned at the same time as the Roman Empire expanded to encompass Britain. It raised a question: Were these forts independently constructed to protect one community from a neighbouring community, or where they part of a co-ordinated effort to protect West Cornwall, and in particular the Land's End and Penwith Peninsula?

Having travelled to all of them, I believe the forts were operating in close coordination. I noticed that given the proximity of the forts and the fact that many of them are built at elevation, one location is often in sight of two or three other locations. These sight lines between locations support a planned and coordinated lookout system between the forts. An example of this is Trencrom Hill Fort – from this vantage point the summit Carnsew Hill Fort, Tregonning Hill and St Michael's Mount are all visible. The same is true of Castle an Dinas, which now has a folly built on it from the fortress stone and which is visible from multiple vantage points all over the Peninsula.

The Land's End and Penwith Peninsula is protected on its coastline by the Promontory Forts, and the hill forts of Trencrom, Castle Pencair and St Michael's Mount had full visibility of any approach over land from the east. Essentially no force could enter the Peninsula without passing one of these locations and being seen, and together they formed three sentinels that had an overview of this land crossing.

In considering the ancient tin and copper trading, I believe that Mount's Bay and St Michael's Mount were locations that the forts were strategically coordinated to protect. The hill forts at Sancreed Beacon, Caer Bran, Castle an Dinas, Trencrom, Tregonning Hill and Lecudjack all have sight lines through to St Michael's Mount and Mount's Bay. Effectively an alarm raised in any of these locations could be relayed quickly to all of the other forts.

It all speaks to a co-ordinated effort, which then raised a follow-on question of why? Why would this part of Cornwall need to be so well defended?

For the most part the fort locations had no immediate access to food or water and were completely exposed to the elements – they were not locations chosen for comfort or convenience. After visiting several of the forts and castles in the winter months, when the wind was howling, the cold was taking hold, and the rain was coming in sideways at force, I could not imagine anyone living there on a permanent basis.

On my visit to nearby Trencrom, I was staggered by the size of rocks used in the perimeter walls of the hill fort, which stretch over one kilometre around the perimeter of the hill. Some of the boulders were as large as cars and I found myself wondering how these ancient people were able to get these huge rocks into position without the aid of modern cranes. When I reached the summit on what was a sunny day the wind gusts were so strong that you really had to lean forward and brace yourself against them. On a separate visit to Chun Castle the weather had been wet and the paths up the hill were rutted and at times ponded. It was heavy going up this elevated section and the climb took some time from the base. As I climbed, the clouds and misty weather were drifting over the top of the hill, giving the place an eerie feel. As I approached the summit I saw the substantial perimeter defensive wall, built out of boulders that do not appear to have come from the hill itself. Perhaps they were quarried elsewhere, but as I stood there catching my breath I couldn't help but wonder how these thousands of stones were brought up the hill and placed to form not one, but two defensive perimeter walls.

Given the sheer scale, these Iron Age forts must have been built by large groups who exerted great effort to build their fortresses. The forts were either a place of retreat, or a secure location for the most valuable treasures of each tribe, or both. It was not only the construction of the fort that required great effort, given their barren location on sea cliffs or at the top of the highest hills; all provisions such as water, food and firewood would have to be brought in. This would have required a level of coordination, planning and cooperation that point to an intelligent and civilised society.

There was clearly a threat that needed to be defended against, but the magnitude of what was built would make no sense in an agricultural setting. Certainly, there would be no need to build such elaborate defences to protect a potato crop or a few cows. And as I had observed travelling in all weathers on the Land's End and Penwith Peninsula, the exposed areas were not the most hospitable of areas to live in, particularly when the weather is bad. Better to go inland and up country to find some pleasant valley, with nearby rivers, to live and survive.

We know there was treasure in this part of Cornwall and that was the rich deposits of copper and tin. Could this be what the forts were storing and defending? We also know that mining and trading of ore was taking place from an early age, and therefore the logical conclusion points strongly in one direction: these forts were constructed to protect the mining operations in the area and to safeguard the ore that was mined, until it was traded.

The promontory forts also signify that the area also needed to be protected from sea attack and their construction also supports the belief that West Cornwall was trading tin and copper during the Bronze and Iron Ages. While we can still see some of the mine engine houses and stacks that were built in the eighteenth and nineteenth century, the countryside is peppered with disused mine shafts and quarries that we cannot see. These unmarked mines were worked long before the advent of steam driven engines, and consequently had no need of engine houses. Within the area there is extensive signage warning of the dangers of straying from footpaths in bracken and foliage covered land, and a brief look at the Ordnance Survey map 102 for Land's End, Penzance and St Ives shows, in part, the extent of these disused mines, shafts and quarries. For every mine building that we can see today, there were many more mine shafts that had been in operation since ancient times.

PROMONTORY FORTS

Treryn Dinas

Situated on the south coast of the Land's End and Penwith Peninsula near the Logan Rock and the village of Treen is Treryn Dinas. This fort, which is also referred to as a castle, is an Iron Age Promontory Fort, and is on the coastline protected by cliffs on three of its sides. After parking in the village of Treen, I followed a footpath that led across a number of farmer's fields with stone stiles between them. The directional signs in the village refer to Logan Rock, which was a large eight tonne rock that was finely balanced on a cliff top, and could be moved slightly by hand pressure. This is the attraction in the area rather that the fort itself, but as the rock is next to the fort, all paths lead to the same place. Infamously the rock was pushed off its seat by Naval Lieutenant Goldsmith in 1824, which sent it crashing down. The locals were naturally in uproar and the Admiralty ordered Lieutenant Goldsmith to recover the stone and place it in its original location at his own expense. Replacing the stone proved to be a major venture involving teams of men, ropes and tackle to lift it back to the top of the cliff, and while they managed to do this, it is reported that it has never rocked the way it did before the incident. As I left the village of Treen and headed south, the seascape began to open up and I saw the Scillonian ferry making its journey back from the Isles of Scilly to its harbour in Penzance. The fields were full of vegetables growing in dark fertile soil, and I wondered how it was that in and amongst the rocky craggy landscape of the peninsula there were such large tracts of beautifully rich soil. At the bottom of the fields I crossed the south-west Cornwall coastal path, and then up a slight hill where I found the entrance was signposted with a marker fixed to a granite rock, 'Treryn Dinas Iron Age cliff castle'.

From this elevated point access to Logan Rock involves a descent down part of the cliff and then an ascent. To the west of the site is Pedn Vender beach and Porthcurno Beach, and the Minack Theatre is within sight on the next western promontory.

Protected on its eastern, western and southern flanks by cliffs, the fort was approachable only from the north. There are a series of ramparts and ditches that were used to defend this approach from any attacker, and these are still visible. Treryn Dinas was one of the largest, if not the largest, of the promontory forts, with a sizeable area of useable land upon on the summit of the cliff.

In 1811 the painter Joseph Mallord William Turner (1775 – 1851) toured Cornwall and sketched Treryn Dinas with Porthcurno in the distance. His visit lasted several weeks, and he made a collection of sketches from different locations in West Cornwall, including Mount's Bay, Gulval, Penzance, Land's End and from Castle an Dinas, a hillfort located to the north of Penzance with striking views across Mount's

Bay and St Michael's Mount. He was clearly taken with Treryn Dinas, making several sketches including a detail of the nearby Logan Rock.

Gurnards Head (Trereen Dias)

Trereen Dias was an Iron Age promontory fort located at Gurnards Head on the north coast of the Land's End and Penwith Peninsula between the villages of Zennor and Morvah. The castle fort is dated to around 2 BC and has two stone ramparts and ditches, and sixteen round houses on the east side of the headland. This was one of the more accessible promontory forts for me to reach with parking relatively nearby, and a short enjoyable walk from the village of Treen down over the fields towards the sea. Treryn Dinas near the village of Treen on the south coast and Trereen Dias near the village of Treen on the north coast are two completely separate places, despite the similarity in place names.

Maen Cliff Castle

Maen Cliff Castle is an Iron Age promontory fort or cliff castle located just over one kilometre to the north of Land's End.

I visited Maen Cliff Castle one blustery November afternoon and after parking at Land's End set off on the short walk, heading northward on the coastal footpath. The sea views from the cliff tops and the interesting rock formations made it an enjoyable stroll, and off the coast at Land's End the Longships Lighthouse was in sight. The land and attractions at Land's End are in private ownership, but Maen Cliff Castle is now part of the National Trust and was well signposted. As I approached the settlement, the coastal path dipped into a hollow and I turned left onto the path leading up to the castle. As I walked up this narrow incline there was a stone rampart marking the entrance into Maen Cliff Castle, which would also have been the critical area of defence in the event of any attack. The outcrop of land on which the castle was located has a small flat summit and then slopes steeply towards the sea. I ventured further into the site, but the north and south sides had very steep falls, before running off the cliff edge, and so I ventured down the west slope, furthest from the entrance. Here I was able to travel a hundred yards or so before the slope became too steep to safely walk on, and with the wind blowing I did not want to be anywhere near the edge. Looking back up the slope towards the entrance it seemed to me that the bulk of the fort's buildings must have been in this narrow sloping location since everywhere else would have been quite precarious.

The castle, which is a scheduled monument, is believed to have been in use between 400 BC and AD 400. The nearest town to the castle location is Sennen, and since the parish church was established in AD 520 it seems probable that the inhabitants of Maen Cliff Castle moved inland at some point between the two dates.

Cape Cornwall

Located on the north-west of the Land's End and Penwith Peninsula, Cape Cornwall closely rivals Land's End for being the most westerly point in Great Britain. The two locations are within sight of each other and Cape Cornwall may have been the site of a fort during the Iron Age or earlier. There is some conjecture as to whether Cape Cornwall was a promontory fort or not. The antiquarian Dr William Borlase speculated that it was, but there is little evidence of defensive structures or remains of settlements on its land side.

The remains of pottery found on the site date back to the late Iron Age period.

I reached Cape Cornwall after passing through the centre of the mining town of St Just and following the sign off the main road. As I travelled out from the town, the road narrowed and twisted down towards the sea. On the left I passed Cape Cornwall golf course and at the bottom of the hill, in direct view of the cape, was a very convenient National Trust car park. From there I set out for the promontory which was a relatively easy walk with gentle climbs. The views of the rugged headland and the swells of the Atlantic were magnificent, and just to the north-east two small islands named 'The Brisons' come into view, isolated in the deep blue sea about a kilometre offshore.

The monument at the summit of Cape Cornwall has a plaque that records the purchase of Cape Cornwall by H J Heinz Company for the nation and its gift to the National Trust on March 25, 1987, the centennial year of the company. The small stone building at the base of Cape Cornwall is the Medieval St Helen's Oratory, which replaced a sixth century church.

On a separate visit to the nearby National Trust site of Carn Gloose to see the Ballowall Barrow, a Bronze Age funerary monument, I realized the two locations were next to each other and the view from Carn Gloose looked out onto Cape Cornwall. The two sites were connected on a short hill road and can easily be viewed together. The barrow is an impressive ancient monument about sixty metres in diameter and two metres tall, built with thousands of granite rocks intricately weaved together. According to the National Trust, the barrow dates to the late Neolithic Period. It occurred to me that to have gone to so much effort to build an impressive burial chamber there must have been a large settlement of people in the area. Given the close proximity of Cape Cornwall, and the natural defence it would offer as a promontory fort, it did seem likely that this was once the location of ancient settlement of people.

Carn Les Boel

The Iron Age Promontory Fort at Carn Les Boel is situated a short distance south of Land's End, just off of the coastal footpath between Mill Bay and Pendower Cove on the south-west of the peninsula. Two large stones indicate the entrance to the fort, although the site is heavily weathered, which is hardly surprising given its exposure to the Atlantic Ocean. This location is close to Gwennap Head, the location that had the highest wind speed ever recorded in England. There are no visible remains of any settlement on the promontory, but its protection from attack on the sea sides are obvious as is the restricted access from the land side. The site is a scheduled monument under the Ancient Monuments and Architectural Area Act 1979.

Kenidjack Cliff Castle

Kenidjack Cliff Castle is located under two kilometres east of Cape Cornwall on a promontory overlooking the sea and Kenidjack Valley. A scheduled monument, Kenidjack is within the parish of St Just and the entrance to the valley is opposite the village of Tregeseal. This was one of the most enjoyable walks on my visits to the promontory forts, as the trail from the Tregeseal Junction follows a stream down into a deep valley and the sound of the water stays with you throughout. Bordered on either side by hills, the stream runs through the undergrowth and emerges at several small rocky pools and waterfalls. As you descend into the valley the granite stone remnants of the Kenidjack mining district come into view, and this includes several well-preserved structures and an exceptionally high chimney stack. The ore in this area was found in deep mine shafts and was processed on the surface by rock crushing stamps and calciners that burnt off the arsenic contaminants on the ore. These granite buildings continue down the trail and I could imagine the area as a small industrial village when it was operational. Since this was an historic mining centre there are piles of mine spoilings on either side of the path down to the sea, some are so steep that retaining walls have been built to hold them in place. The promontory fort area comes into view lower down the trail and at the bottom of the path the stream opens up to the coast. It was a magnificent sight with the waves rolling in across the bay and Cape Cornwall with its monument on the opposite side.

From the seaside of Kenidjack Promontory Fort I walked around the lower part of the cliffs on a small narrow path, and looking up I could see that the steepness of the cliff sides would have made the fort impenetrable from the sea. The whole area is now part of the National Trust and the fort site dates back to the Iron Age and possibly earlier. The land side and entrance on to the promontory is protected by three ramparts with ditches.

Bosigran Castle

Bosigran Castle is located on the north coastal footpath between the towns of Morvah and Zennor. Just one and a half kilometres to the south east is Men An Tol, an ancient stone monument. This Iron Age castle on the promontory was separated from the headland by a dry stone wall, and is protected by Porthmoina Bay on its west side and Haldrine Cove on its east. The location is within sight of Gurnards Head, and a common theme of the promontory forts is that they were either in sight of each other or could be alerted quickly if an alarm was raised. The castle is a Scheduled Monument and is now part of the National Trust, and can be accessed from the nearby National Trust site of Carn Galver Mine. There is a small car park next to the mine and this is just off the roadside on the Zennor to Morvah stretch of the B3306. After parking I set off past the substantial remains of the Carn Galver mine, heading down the hill towards the coast. The trail to the east of the mine through the trees was incredibly rocky, and not just rocks on the surface of a flat path, but rocks embedded into the ground and poking out. In places I was hopping between stones as I would have done crossing a rocky beach. As the woodland opened up the path improved, and I could see all the way down to the coastline with the Cornish coastal path also in view. The area is still farmed and there were groups of inquisitive cows that I passed by on the way.

This location on the sea front is steeped in history and the National Trust map identifies Bronze Age and Iron Age fields, which like so many in the area are formed by granite dry stone walls. The remains of the old mining stamp houses of Bosigran and Porthmoina are also nearby, and the whole walk is overshadowed by the summit of Carn Galver standing at two hundred and twenty metres above sea level. When walking back up the hill the granite mine shells and the peak of Carn Galver dominate the landscape. As I reflected on the tranquil surroundings and picturesque views, it seemed to me that this location would have been far busier in ancient times and when mining was in full production than it is now. Carn Galver mine had operated between 1830 and 1878 and the nearby mining Carn Galver Count House still exists as 'The Climbers Club'.

The National Trust sign at the car park included a story about the author D.H. Lawrence, who lived with his German wife Frieda near Zennor. During the First World War they were accused of signalling to German U Boats and on a separate occasion when a light was seen at the Carn Galver Count House in 1917, a police raid found the couple singing German songs with the tenant Mr Cecil Gray. It seems that Gray was fined for breaking the blackout regulations and D.H. Lawrence and his wife were expelled from Cornwall. Frieda Lawrence was the cousin of Manfred Albrecht Freiherr von Richtofen, otherwise known as the Red Baron.

HILL FORTS

While the promontory forts helped protect the Land's End and Penwith Peninsula from coastal attack, there were further and more substantial defences built inland:

Trencrom

Trencrom is an Iron Age hill fort with extensive defensive features and is situated on Trencrom Hill, to the west of Hayle and south of St Ives. The hill is visible from distance on the A30 at the western approach near Hayle. At one-hundred-and-seventy-five metres above sea level it is not a mountain, but is given prominence as it is surrounded to the east and south by low lying land. There is a National Trust car park part of the way up Trencrom Hill, and the hill can also be accessed from the nearby village of Trencrom. From either location it is a short walk to the boundary of the fortifications, and of all the forts I visited in Cornwall this defence wall is the most impressive not only in length, but in the size of the boulders used to form the perimeter boundary. This defensive wall is some fifty metres lower than the summit of the hill and is over one kilometre long and made up of huge stone boulders. Still intact, it would have been impenetrable to an attacking force during battle. There are areas to pass through the defensive wall and from there I climbed up to the summit.

The views from the top of the hill are far reaching and panoramic and I could see right across the Cornish countryside to Mount's Bay and St Michael's Mount. As I swept my view from south to north, both Godolphin Hill and Tregonning Hill were in view in the east, and Hayle estuary and the coastline to Godrevy Lighthouse stood out in the north. With these views Trencrom was ideally situated as a hill fort, and in the far distance even Cairn Euny in Redruth is in sight.

As I looked around the summit there was limited flat area within the fort and I could only assume that the hill slopes were also used for living quarters. Around the summit and slightly lower down were huge stone structures that as far as I could tell appeared to be man-made. There is some suggestion that the Iron Age fort on Trencrom Hill may have had an earlier Neolithic settlement. Penlee House Gallery & Museum in Penzance has several leaf shaped arrowheads and flint scrapers dating from between 4,000 – 2,500 BC, which were found near Trencrom Hill.

Having visited several forts I always ask myself the question – how would the inhabitants have been able to feed and water themselves? In this case the land surrounding Trencrom is currently used for grazing cattle, and there are wells on the sides of the hill that would have provided water for the fort's inhabitants. In this regard it would have been easier to have maintained a settlement at Trencrom compared to some of the other forts.

To the west of Trencrom is a disused tin mine, which was known as Wheal Cherry before being renamed as Trencrom Mine and Mount Lane Mine. Its granite engine house and chimney stack stand out against the green rolling hills.

Trencrom Hill and fort is now part of the National Trust and a plaque at the top of the hill narrates that Trencrom was presented to the National Trust by Lt. Col. G. L. Tryringham of Trevethoe in March 1946. In my view the site is the best example of a defensive hill fort within the area and it retains many of its features. To see first-hand the size of the boulders used in the wall defences and to think about how they were placed in position, makes Trencrom definitely worth a visit.

Caer Bran

An Iron Age hill fort half a mile west of the ancient village of Carn Euny, which is administered by English Heritage. This hill fort is over one hundred and ninety metres above sea level and has commanding views over the surrounding countryside. The earth ramparts built for the defence of the fort are still visible.

Chun Castle

Located at two-hundred-and-fifteen metres above sea level, Chun Castle has far reaching views over the surrounding countryside. Located south of Morvah, the site was an Iron Age Castle Fort with two circular perimeter stone walls. These walls are still in place, together with large standing stones marking the castle's entrance points. If the stone used for the walls was not mined from the top of the hill, and there is no immediate evidence that it was, then the stone must have been brought in and carried up the hill.

The construction of the castle on top of a high, steep sided hill, would have been a major physical undertaking requiring a critical mass of people to support the construction. Life at the summit of the hill would have been hard, the heavy bracken and gorse bushes surrounding the castle would have ruled out any immediate area to farm or graze cattle. The support of a community within the castle would have required careful planning and organization, with separation of responsibilities for farming, cattle herding, weapon production, look out, water transportation and maintaining the defences. In fact, it would have been a huge demand on the occupants' resources to build the castle and then keep it functional. It was not the best of days when I visited, and the weather had closed in, but in another way it added to the atmosphere on the summit, with the low cloud and mist drifting in and out of the stones.

Chun Castle was believed to be in use between the third century BC until the first century AD and is a short walk to the much older Chun Quoit.

Sancreed Beacon

Sancreed is close to the centre of the Land's End and Penwith Peninsula and almost equidistant between the towns of Newlyn and St Just. Sancreed Beacon is located to the west of the village and sits atop of Sancreed Hill which is over one-hundred-and-eighty metres high. There is provision for parking next to Beacon on the Sancreed to St Just road, and the site has an information board and location map at the entrance point. It was a gentle climb from the entrance to the summit, and the views were far reaching in all directions, including down to Mount's Bay and St Michael's Mount. The hill fort at Caer Bran is less than one-and-a-half kilometres away to the south-west, and beyond is the village of St Buryan with its distinctive Parish Church. Beyond St Buryan is the southern coastline and the sea beyond.

As I studied the summit it seemed that whatever stone wall defences there had been were largely lost to time and the elements. There was a small stone wall that gave an indication of what may have been the outer defence wall. Given the location and the views it is certain to have been a settlement at some point. At the lower points of the hill there were disused mine shafts and more were noted on the site location map than on the Ordnance Survey. I'm sure local knowledge prevails in this case, but it did make me wonder just how many abandoned and unmarked mine shafts there are in Cornwall.

The same day I visited the Parish Church and concluded that the village of Sancreed is a good example of how different generations came together from the ancient times and their hill forts, later developing open ground mining and the driving of mine shafts without the engine buildings and tower stacks of the nineteenth century. The construction of the Parish Church dates to the thirteenth to fifteenth centuries and the village is still flourishing through to the present.

Castle-an-Dinas

Located less than three kilometres east of the village of Ludgvan, Castle-an-Dinas was an ancient hill fort located two-hundred and thirty-three-metres above sea level. Although it can be seen for miles around, it is quite a challenge getting to the top. The footpath to the summit is opposite the junction of the B3309, the road heading west from the village of Ludgvan, at its intersection with the B3311, Penzance to St Ives road. There is nothing to signpost the footway that passes between a row of houses other than the clue given in the name of the area, which is called Castle Gate. The footpath was narrow and a little overgrown with summer vegetation immediately after leaving the road, but opened up after a few hundred metres. Although the footpath starts in a direct line with the top of the hill, it diverts to the left until you arrive at the entrance of Castle-an-Dinas quarry. This quarry is active and operates a large opencast mine for stone aggregate. From here the footpath crosses the entrance road to the quarry with its offices and heavy machinery on the other side of a secure fence and gate. And after turning sharp right the path is then diverted around the south and east of the quarry operations with its vast hills of graded aggregate ready to be dispatched. This circular journey takes you around a significant portion of the hill and then upwards on to the summit.

At the peak is the Rogers Tower, a two-storey castle-like structure that can be seen from miles around. This tower is classified as a folly, a Scheduled Monument and is a Grade II listed building. Its construction is attributed to John Rogers (1750 – 1832) who lived on the Penrose Estate, near Loe Bar, south of Helston. John Rogers was a lawyer and politician, and represented West Looe, Penryn and Helston as a Member of Parliament. The folly was built in the eighteenth-century and one source places it at 1798. The antiquarian Dr Borlase (1696 – 1772) and rector of nearby Ludgvan Church, visited and inspected Castle-an-Dinas, and afterward noted that the diameter of the fort was four hundred feet and that a third circular wall was partially built. The two men may have met, and perhaps had a shared interest in Castle-an-Dinas. They do, however, have a common connection with St Paul Parish Church in Ludgvan. Historic England have a registry for Rogers Chest, which is a Grade II listed tomb located 'east of south aisle of Church at St Paul', in Ludgvan. The inscription is recorded 'To John Rogers of Treassowe and of Penrose ac Sithney 1750 – 1832 and Margaret widow of the above died 1842'. Treassowe is equidistant between Ludgvan and Castle-an-Dinas and the inscription informs us that John Rogers lived in the shadow of the hill within the parish of Ludgvan. From this location he would have been close to and would have seen the tower on the hill.

The hillfort location is impressive; from the summit there were views down to Mount's Bay and along the coastline past Perranuthnoe. It was from this location in 1811 that Joseph Mallord William Turner sketched Mount's Bay and St Michael's Mount when visiting Cornwall. What I had not realised until I had visited was that the other views were equally impressive. Looking north I could see Towednack Parish Church in the foreground with its distinctive short tower, and beyond was Zennor Hill, Trendrine Hill and Rosewall Hill. In between theses landmarks, the blue seas on the north coast came into sight, forming v shapes between the hills. Sweeping my gaze around to the north-east there was Trink Hill and close by was Trencrom Hillfort just three-and-a-half kilometres away. Castle-an-Dinas is sixty metres higher than Trencrom, which allowed a view of the hillfort summit. Between Trink Hill and Trencrom the Porthkidney Sands at Hayle estuary could also be seen in the distance.

To the east and slightly south were Godolphin Hill and Tregonning Hill, and to the west the prominent Ding Dong mine stood out on its hill ridge just over four kilometres away. This location is said to be one of the earliest mining centres and it is surrounded by several of the ancient monuments, such as Men an Tol and Lanyon Quoit.

Historic England register Castle-an-Dinas as a 'small multivallate hill-fort' and define this term as referring to a fortified enclosure between one and five hectares in size, dating back to the Iron Age. From my visit there was nothing that stood out as fortifications, but as you make your way through the bracken paths below the peak the perimeter stone walls can be seen. These walls are low and covered in vegetation, and there is a warning sign for the old mine shafts in the area. The hillfort site at Castle-an-Dinas is estimated to be over one hectare, or approximately eleven thousand square metres. At this size a circular fort would have a diameter of one-hundred-and-twenty metres and a circumference approaching four-hundred-metres. This size seemed quite compatible with the flattish area at the summit, and in the normal sense was not really small at all. As I stood there and looked out I felt this location was central to the hill forts, and apart from the connectivity to the hillforts I have mentioned above it was also possible to see Sancreed Beacon in the distance on the west of the Land's End and Penwith Peninsula.

To avoid the long detour around the quarry and repeating the outward journey, I headed east down the hill ridge in the direction of Castle Gate. The open pit of the quarry had been visible from the hill, but I was seeking a more direct detour around the mine excavations to the north. At the perimeter fence it was incredible to see how deep the mine excavations had gone down, and the sheer granite faces that marked the furthest edges of the quarry. I skirted around the perimeter first heading north, but then heading west and in the opposite direction to the way I had hoped to go. The access points that I passed were all marked 'Private Land', and in the end I was forced to head back to the summit and retrace the footpath I had travelled earlier. At one intersection on the footpath there is another path that heads south with Chysauster Ancient Village just five hundred metres away. Since both locations were in operation at the same time it seems that the two communities would have supported each other in some way.

Lescudjack Castle

Located on the eastern hillside of Penzance, Lescudjack Castle was a relatively small hill fort, but strategically important as the fort closest to Mount's Bay. It is easy to pass by the location of the castle, which is close to the A30 above Chyandour, without knowing it is there. There are no signposts giving directions to the castle, and I only found it after driving through Penzance residential streets. Urbanisation has over the years seen residences encroach up to and around the castle site. Once I arrived at the correct location there was a nice stone sign elegantly carved with the inscription 'Lescudjack Castle Hillfort'. The site is nothing more than a field now, and if it were not for the sign at the entrance, I would have put the location down as a small park between residential streets.

From the entrance I could only see the grassy field above me, but as I walked up the hill and reached the centre I was able to witness the castle's commanding views over Mount's Bay, all the way from Mousehole to the promontory near Perranuthnoe. Within the view was St Michael's

Mount, a few kilometres to the south-west, as well as views down to the town of Penzance. The castle would have formed a base to protect the shores of Mount Bay, but did not benefit from views into the interior of the Land's End and Penwith Peninsula. Despite its seemingly forgotten status Lescudjack Castle is a Scheduled Monument.

Carnsew

Carnsew Hill Fort is a scheduled monument located near the Hayle river estuary. These days the estuary is silted over, but in the past, it was a major route for shipping to Lelant or Hayle. Carnsew Hill Fort was situated on the south side of the estuary and would have had clear views of all shipping going in or out of the estuary.

Historical records for this period of time are non-existent and only the remains of the ancient Promontory and Hill Fort structures are left to speak to us. And they do speak of an industrious people, who were highly organized. Since we know from the historian Diodorus Siculas that the Cornish, and in particular the West Cornish, were trading in tin from before 60 BC, the presence of these defensive structures does, in my opinion, provide strong evidence of tin trading for hundreds and possibly thousands of years prior to this. Who were the traders? Well I believe the Phoenicians were strong candidates, most likely surpassed by the Greeks and Romans, when Phoenicia was overrun.

ANCIENT VILLAGES

Carn Euny

Located near the village of Sancreed on the Land's End and Penwith Peninsula, Cairn Uny is a late Iron Age settlement. The site is of particular interest as it has stone structures both above and below ground level. The elements of the settlement above ground consist of a number of round clusters with perimeter walls. Built on the side of a hill the settlement has panoramic views out to the western side of the Land's End and Penwith Peninsula.

After viewing the areas above ground I reached the entrance to the underground fogou and circular chamber, which I found at the higher end of the settlement. An opening between two walls led to me to the stone steps that descended from ground level down to the underground structures. At this lower level there was a passage-way that led to a circular round chamber, enclosed on all sides with large stone blocks. I found that it was possible to stand completely upright and estimated that the chamber was about four metres in diameter. Despite being underground, light was able to penetrate from above, highlighting the green algae on the stone walls. Adjacent to the chamber is an underground passageway or tunnel, known as a fogou, and this was approximately ten metres long with light and foliage visible at its end. As I looked along the fogou I realised that I would need to be on all fours, to pass through the low-level square tunnel. It occurred to me that it was possibly an escape route and alternative exit from the underground sections.

Excavations at Carn Euny indicate that the site was in use during the Neolithic Period. The term Neolithic was coined by Sir John Lubbock (1834 – 1913) to cover the overlapping period within the late stone age and bronze age and ended around 2,500 BC. Sir John Lubbock became Baron Avebury and during his time as a Member of Parliament he introduced The Ancient Monuments Protection Act of 1882. He is better remembered now for bringing in the Bank Holidays Act of 1871, which provided for the first-time statutory holidays for all workers.

Carn Euny is one of many properties that are administered by English Heritage, and the information boards provided on the site gave detailed information about the settlement. The site has been in use for thousands of years and is near rich fertile agricultural land, which is still being actively farmed today. Two hundred metres to the west of Carn Euny is a well, which would have provided for the settlement.

Chysauster Ancient Village

This is one of the best-preserved ancient villages that can be visited and is also under the administration of English Heritage.

This elevated settlement is a collection of 10 large dwellings, known as courtyard houses with a common driveway between them. The houses were constructed of stone and are remarkably well preserved given that they date back two thousand years. The dwelling walls are largely intact and would have had thatched roofs over the living quarters. Part of the site is described as a likely location of an ore smelter, which indicates that mining was already established in this part of West Cornwall.

It is believed that the settlement was inhabited from 100 BC making it a late Iron Age village. The Romans invaded England in AD 43 when Chysauster was still a working village and it remained so for another one hundred and fifty years. Like other ancient settlements, Chysauster is at elevation, towards the top of a very steep hill. Being slightly lower than the summit gave the village better shelter against the wind, but the height on the hill still provided an early warning of anyone approaching and a strong defence against any attacks. I was impressed by how organised the village layout was and it is easy to imagine the ancient community working and living in the spacious, well built stone dwellings, enjoying the views across the countryside and down to Mount's Bay.

There are other ancient villages on the Land's End and Penwith Peninsula including Bodrifty, Busullow, Trehylis, Bosporthennis and Mulfra Vean.

ANCIENT MONUMENTS

Lanyon Quoit

Lanyon Quoit is just to the side of the road between Morvah on the north Cornish coast and Madron. I don't know how many times I have driven this road and gone past the quoit without noticing it. It is for the large part hidden behind a stone wall, which is overgrown with vegetation. Once I had located Lanyon Quoit I realised how close it was to the road, and that you can catch glimpses of it as you pass by.

The purpose of quoits is not clear; there is some speculation that they may have been used as a burial chamber or to mark a burial site. Quoits appear to be amongst the oldest of the ancient monuments. I wondered if the impressive quoit might have been an art form that publicly displayed the ability of its constructors. How they were assembled is another mystery – the stones would have had to have been carefully chosen and then transported to the place where they would be erected. Given the size of the stones the transportation alone would have taken careful planning and execution, and how the upper stone was placed in position is another question as it is extremely large and incredibly heavy.

Lanyon Quoit has three support stones to carry a stone slab that is estimated to weigh twelve tonnes. There is a 1769 etching by William Borlase which shows a much taller arrangement with different support stone positions. This is because the quoit collapsed in 1815 during a storm and was re-erected in 1816.

Seven hundred metres to the west are the remains of another quoit known as West Lanyon Quoit. Both quoits are believed to be Neolithic and therefore earlier than 2500 BC.

Lanyon Quoit features in the Granada TV series The Return of Sherlock Holmes, where the late Jeremy Brett, who played Sherlock Holmes, is seen by the quoit and other locations in Cornwall during filming of the episode *The Devil's Foot* (1988). Sir Arthur Conan Doyle wrote the short story under the slightly different title 'The Adventure of the Devil's Foot,' and it was published in 1910. Within the story, which is set in Cornwall, Dr Watson describes the place and the thoughts of Sherlock Holmes:

> *In every direction upon these moors there were traces of some vanished race which had passed utterly away, and left as its sole record strange monuments of stone, irregular mounds which contained the burned ashes of the dead, and curious earthworks which hinted at prehistoric strife. The glamour and mystery of the place, with its sinister atmosphere of forgotten nations, appealed to the imagination of my friend, and he spent much of the time in long walks and solitary meditations upon the moor. The ancient Cornish language had also arrested his attention, and he had, I remember, conceived the idea that it was akin to Chaldean, and had been largely derived from the Phoenician traders in tin.*

While the work is fictional, it does give us an insight into the thoughts of Sir Arthur Conan Doyle.

Chun Quoit

Chun Quoit is a short walk from Chun Castle and it did not take many steps before it came into view. The Quoit is reported to have been erected in the Neolithic period around 2,500 BC, which makes it 4,500 years old and still standing. The quoit has a large rounded stone top and is supported by four vertically placed stones. Quoits normally have three vertical supports to provide a resting point for the slab, and when three supports are used all points will come in contact with the upper structure. When four supports are used it must be accomplished with great accuracy, and the tops of the stones must be level to ensure they are all in contact with the slab being supported. The four supports make Chun Quoit unusual and as it is an enclosed quoit, this may indicate that it was a burial chamber.

From the quoit there are views from the hill over to Penwith and Morvah on the north coast, and out to sea.

There are other Quoits at:

Zennor Quoit – located south of Zennor.

Sperris Quoit – located two hundred metres from Zennor Quoit.

Mulfra Quoit – located two and a half kilometres from Men an Tol, between the villages of Treen and Newmill, close to Gear Hill.

The Merry Maidens

The Merry Maidens are located just off of the B3315 between Newlyn and Treen, and there is a convenient parking spot right next to the field where the stones are. As I passed through a gate into the field I could immediately see the standing stones above me on a slight incline. The Merry Maidens are nineteen stones laid out to form a circle, within a larger grass expanse. The inner side of each stone has a flat surface, and the stones are recorded as being from the Neolithic period. The reason for the construction of the stone circle is not known, possibly it was ceremonial or a boundary marker. Several hundred metres to the north-east are two impressive standing stones known as 'The Pipers'. These standing stones are within sight of each other and are over four metres high. The local myth is that there were nineteen maidens dancing to music on the sabbath and they were turned to stone. The two pipers were the musicians, who suffered a similar fate. Also close by and on the roadside is the Tregiffian Burial Chamber, a Bronze Age stone tomb.

There are also stone circles at:

> Boskednan or Nine Maidens – less than one-kilometre east of Men an Tol.

> Tregeseal – less than one kilometre east of Botallack.

> Boscawen-Un Stone Circle – less than two kilometres north of St Buryan.

Men An Tol

Men an Tol is located a fifteen-minute walk from the Morvah to Madron road, just to the north of Lanyon Quoit. By the side of the road there is a layby and from the layby I headed east on a footpath that passes by Busullow Common. After about half a kilometre there was an old farm on the left of the path that had a maze of dry-stone walls separating its pasture-land. I don't know how old these walls are, but I felt sure they were not recently built. Some of the farm buildings were derelict and the farmhouse itself looked empty and abandoned. After another ten minutes of walking a set of stone steps appeared on the right of the path and once over these Men an Tol is in sight. There are three stones: two upright and a centre circular stone with a circle cut in its centre. Recorded as being from the Bronze Age, the arrangement appears to have been altered since the time it was drawn by the antiquarian William

Borlase in the eighteenth century. The area immediately around Men an Tol has a number of other monuments and standing stones, and as with Lanyon Quoit, it is in sight of Ding Dong mine.

Other nearby ancient monuments include crosses, wells and tombs such as Madron Well, Venton Bebibell Well, Tregiffian Burial Chamber, Bosiliack Barrow and Ballowal Barrow.

Standing Stones

There are hundreds of standing stones in West Cornwall. The standing stones range in sizes and shapes, and can be isolated from surrounding objects or attached to stone walls. The standing stones in West Cornwall that are included below are large upright pieces of granite, which were believed to have served different purposes. The stones may have marked a place of ceremonial gathering or a burial area – they may also have been a location marker or point marking territory between different groups:

The Pipers – located near Boleigh just off of the B3315. These are two large standing stones separated from each other by several hundred metres. One stone is vertical, the other is at an incline. Since they are near the Merry Maidens legend has it that the two locations are linked.

Men Scryfa – this is an inscribed standing stone less than four hundred metres from Men an Tol. The inscription is in Roman and reads *Rialobrani Cunovali Fili,* which translates to Rialobranus, son of Cunovalus. This is just one of a few pointers to the Romans in Cornwall.

Tresvennack – over three and a half metres tall, located north of Mousehole near Kerris.

In the past there have been discoveries of gold objects dated to the Bronze Age near Towednack and Morvah on the north of the Land's

End and Penwith Peninsula. These treasures were taken to the British Museum for display and safekeeping.

It also seems possible that whoever was trading tin and copper with the inhabitants of West Cornwall would have stationed their own representatives on land to coordinate the trading and shipments. Perhaps it was these trading ambassadors that helped organise the defensive forts and castles to store and protect the tin stocks?

ROMANS, SAXONS, VIKINGS AND NORMANS

THE ABANDONMENT OF ANCIENT SITES coincided with Roman rule in Great Britain between AD 43 – AD 410. The reason for this is really subject to some conjecture, but we could assume that the threat, which the inhabitants of West Cornwall were defending against, had subsided. This in turn eroded the need for the forts, and there would have been a natural desire to move out of these barren and inhospitable locations. The formation of nearby towns at the end of the Iron Age and beginning of the Middle Ages is evidence of this transition.

Whatever the precise reason, the forts were abandoned and the populace migrated inland away from the extremities of the coastline and the hill forts. The locations that were selected for resettlement were often nearby, as was the case in Sancreed where the modern-day village is located close to the elevated Hill Fort of Sancreed Beacon, but at a lower and more sheltered location.

The Romans' direct rule of Britain came to an end after AD 400, and despite the fact that the Romans occupied Britain for nearly four-hundred years, there was little evidence of them in Cornwall. No major forts or roads were built and there are no records of major battles. In fact, from a Cornish perspective there is little to show that the Romans were ever here at all. I found this a curious fact since the tin and copper trade would have been of great importance to the Romans, and yet they seem not to have directly intervened or aggressively occupied Cornwall.

By inference it is possible to view the Romans' presence in England as facilitating the continuance of the mining and trading of tin, and it must be logical to assume that the Romans were themselves benefiting from the trade, as little could happen in Europe at that time without their approval. At the very least it would seem that Cornwall did not pose a threat to the Roman occupation, and as such, Roman interests were best served in protecting the industry without direct intervention. Since this period of time also ties in with the abandonment of the Promontory and Hill Forts in West Cornwall, this seems to give an impression of safety and security felt on both sides.

When the Romans left England, there was a counter-effect that Dr William Borlase summarised in his Observations on the antiquities historical and monumental of the county of Cornwall. In his work, William Borlase noted of the Roman departure from Britain:

> *The Romans were no sooner retir'd from Britan, than the Scots and the Picts, in hopes of bettering their condition, made frequent inroads from Scotland. The Britans had now, for some ages, been accustomed to recruit the Roman armies abroad, with the choicest of their youths, and*

*being seldom inur'd to bear arms at home, where they had no encourage-
ment, to study the profession of a soldier (their masters, the Romans, for
political reasons, secluding them as much as possible from the art of war)
they found it a very difficult matter after a disuse of so many ages, to
bring themselves to any tolerable relish for the duties of the field . . . The
Britans seeing themselves under these disadvantages, and despairing of
ever being a match for their enemies, whose barbarity they were every
day experiencing, without any hope of ever satisfying their thirst of
spoil, determin'd to call in foreign aid; and the Saxons having been for
some time remarkable at sea, had also by this time got the name of the
most valiant nation on the continent; the Saxons, therefore, then seated
on the German shores opposite to the North-eastern parts of the island,
being a populous nation, soldiers of fortune, and us'd to sea expeditions,
seemed most likely to afford the speedy and effectual assistance, which
the Britans so much wanted.*

William Borlase relates that the Britans had selected Vortigern Earl of
Cornwall as their King between AD 430 and AD 452, and that Vortigern
called upon the Saxons to battle the Scots and Picts. The Saxons took up
this challenge and succeeded where the Britans had failed, and secured
the northern border. Here the intentions of the Saxons changed, and
they chose to stay on in England and take up arms against the people that
had hired them. Worse still, around AD 460 the Saxons murdered three
hundred of the principal British nobility near Salisbury. Having been
called in to assist the Britans following the departure of the Romans, the
Saxons occupied and scattered the Britans, who fled to the west country
and to the south coast of England, before sailing for the continent. It
would seem likely that the links that developed between Brittany and
Normandy in France and Cornwall are due to this migration and a natural desire to maintain close contact. The bond between Mont St Michel

in Normandy and the former priory at St Michael's Mount is an example of this linkage, as are the missionaries who visited West Cornwall.

Cornwall found an unlikely ally in the Danes to repel and fight against the Saxons and this relationship continued over time. William Borlase noted of the Vikings:

'. . . but when they landed in Cornwall they seem'd to have always march'd into Devenshire to fight the Saxons.'

According to William Borlase this alliance lasted more than one hundred years and he intimates that hill castles with the name Dinas in them have a link to the Danes (Dinas – Danes) such as Castle An Dinas. In 838 a combined Cornish and Danish force was defeated by the Saxons at Hingston Down, near Callington, Cornwall. This did not stop the Danes from further skirmishes in the following years, including a siege of Exeter in 1001.

On a visit to the British Museum in London, and in particular the Ancient Britain section, there were a number of beautiful artefacts that represented the period between the end of the Iron Age and the Middle Ages. However, what struck me was that the map showing the area occupied by the Saxons ended at Devon to the west and Scotland to the north. Cornwall was able to defend itself against the Saxon advances and remain independent, the Tamar river giving the degree of separation between the two opposing forces.

King Athelstan (894 – 939), who was both King of the Anglo Saxons and later titled King of the English, led a force into Cornwall. During this campaign he stopped at Saint Buriana's Parish Church in St Buryan to pray. Later, and after his campaign in Cornwall, he issued a charter for the establishment of a monastery in St Buryan.

After this, and with England united under one monarch, the Saxons did infuse their way into Cornwall over the following centuries and we know this from the land ownership records within the Domesday Book. The Domesday Book was an audit of the land ordered by William the Conqueror and was carried out twenty years after he had defeated King Harold at the Battle of Hastings in 1066. As a result of the Norman Conquest and the Domesday Book survey, the Saxons were replaced as landowners in Cornwall. A number of the prominent Cornish families trace their ancestry back to Normandy and initially large parts of Cornwall were given to Robert, Count of Mortain, 2ⁿᵈ Earl of Cornwall (1031-1095), a half-brother of William the Conqueror.

MIDDLE-AGES
THE PARISH CHURCHES WITHIN THE LAND'S END AND PENWITH PENINSULA

FOLLOWING MY VISIT TO TREGONNING HILL and the preaching pit where the visits of John and Charles Wesley were celebrated by a memorial plaque located at the entrance to the small amphitheatre, I decided to research in more detail the visits of John Wesley to Cornwall, and in particular West Cornwall. There was a wealth of material, not only from his daily journals, but also from other sources. I wanted to know the places that he had visited in the area and understand more about the impact that had on the local populace. Although John Wesley took to preaching outdoors in various locations throughout Great Britain and Ireland, he was an ordained minister of the Church of England. It very quickly became apparent to me that in West Cornwall, the locations that John Wesley visited and preached at were, for the most part, towns that had parish churches. Where a local vicar was accommodating he would preach inside the church, and in other circumstances he would preach outside in the churchyard or nearby fields after the main service had finished. The departing churchgoers provided an opportunity for him to maximise the number of people who would hear his message, but he made a point of not disrupting the regular church service, many of which he attended.

From the locations and dates in the journals I wanted to see and visit as many of the parish churches that would have been in existence when John Wesley made his visits to Cornwall, over a period of nearly half a century from 1743. I found that nearly all the parish churches on the Land's End and Penwith Peninsula that are still in existence, were there when John Wesley made his visits, and it became a very tangible link to the past. To step into the doorways and buildings that he had visited on many occasions was like taking a step back into the past. I also came to realise that in looking for buildings that pre-existed the eighteenth century, the parish churches were in a category of their own and provide a visible link to the period that followed the Iron Age in West Cornwall. As I travelled from church to church, there was often some kindly person in attendance, who had given up their time on a voluntary basis to open the door and answer any questions I might have. This seemed to me to be such kind dedication in supporting their local parish church and in doing so allowed visitors, like myself, to access and see these buildings that have been here for centuries. The parish churches had a common thread, with parts of the original construction being preserved, but often with new aisles or towers being added at a later date. This construction over different periods of time was not immediately apparent to the naked eye and, if I had not been told or found it in my research, you could not really tell where the old stopped and the new started – and by new, we are still talking over five hundred years ago in most cases.

The dates of construction for the Parish Churches in West Cornwall also mirror the Middle Ages between AD 500 and AD 1500. They are really the only buildings that we can still see that are younger than the ancient sites and older than the granite mine engine houses and tower stacks that are dotted around the countryside. It is fascinating to think that the Cornish families and individuals mentioned in this book would have seen what we can still see today. Indeed, many of these families were christened and married in these parish churches and would have attended services on a regular basis. In short, the parish churches give us a window back in time, and all of those mentioned in the following chapter were built before the advent of the English Civil War, with some built as early as AD 520.

The names of the parish churches are linked to Irish saints and missionaries, some of whom came to Cornwall in the fifth to sixth centuries, spreading a message of Christianity. It would be natural to think that the visits by these missionaries led to an immediate conversion of the populace to Christianity and the start of a church building programme to honour the missionaries. However, the reality is somewhat darker, with many of the early missionaries being martyred upon their arrival on Cornwall's shores. A number of these missionaries, including Saint Ia, from which we have the town name of St Ives, were executed at Hayle estuary by Cornish King Tewdar, who is also alternatively referred to as King Tewdrig, Theodorick or Tudor.

These executions happened on more than one occasion, According to Dr William Borlase, 'Fingarus with his sister Piala, eleven bishops and a numerous attendance all baptised by St Patrick (who died about 490 AD) came into Cornwall and landing at the mouth of the river Hayle was there to put to death with all his company.'

Sabine Baring-Gould relates the same event and speaks of Fingar (Fingarus):

He brought over with him his sister Kiara, whose name has become Piala or Phillack in Cornish, according to a phoenetic and constant rule. According to legend he had over seven hundred emigrants with him. He and his party made their way from Hayle to Connerton, where they spent the night, and then pushed south to where stands Gwinear. Here Fingar left his party to go ahead and explore. He reached Tregotha, where is a fine spring of water, and there paused to refresh himself, when, hearing cries from behind, he hurried back, and found that Tewdrig, the Cornish king or prince, who lived in Riviere, on a creek in the Hayle river, had hastened after the party of colonists, and had fallen on them and massacred them. When Fingar came up Tewdrig killed him also. Piala the sister does not seem to have been harmed; and as in the long-run the Irish succeeded in establishing themselves firmly in the district, she settled near Riviere and founded the church of Phillack.

Around the same time St Breaca (now called Breague) attended with many saints among who were Sinnius (now called Senanus), the Abbot Germochus and several others They landed off of the estuary near the river Hayle where they were also killed.

According to William Borlase the reason for the terrible executions seems to lie in Tewdar's fear that his subjects would turn from their local religion. It was a barbaric act to kill the missionaries and raises the question why King Tewdar took the course he did. There do seem to be some additional facts in the narratives from S Baring-Gould, Dr William Borlase and other sources which give some additional background. The initial migration it seems was from Ireland to Wales from the late fourth, and early fifth century, and some of the Irish migration to Wales then transferred to Cornwall in the early to mid-fifth century. The kingdom of Osraige in Ireland, also known as Ossory, was between the kingdoms of Leinster and Munster, and in the fifth century it was an early Christian centre. Saint Patrick visited the area frequently and was buried in Kilkenny, which is part of what was once Osraige. S Baring-Gould believes this is where the Irish contingent who sailed to Cornwall came from.

The history of the migration seems to have started with a dispute with its neighbour Munster during the fifth century, Osraige lost part of its territory and its ruling, or royal family was displaced and usurped. The narratives of S Baring-Gould and William Borlase both indicate sizeable groups arriving on the shores of Cornwall, and not just a few missionaries. It is possible that King Tewdar viewed this as an invasion or prelude to a wider invasion into his territory. Also, given that some of the Irish missionaries were part of Irish nobility in their home area, this might also have been viewed by King Tewdar as a direct challenge to his authority.

We know that remnants of the Irish who came to Cornwall in the late fifth and early sixth centuries survived, because we see that many of the place names and parish churches were named after them. In the earlier chapter on Tregonning Hill there were examples of nearby towns and parish churches that were named after these Irish Saints, and other examples on the Land's End and Penwith Peninsula are:

St Ives – Named after St Ia, an Irish missionary of noble birth.

Sennen – Named after St Senanus, an Irish missionary.

St Uny Church Lelant – Named after St Euny (St Uny), an Irish missionary.

Saint Breaca Church, Breage – Named after St Breaca, an Irish missionary.

Gwinear (Nr Hayle) – Named after St Gwinear (Fingar), an Irish missionary.

Saint Pialas Church, Phillack – Named after St Piala, an Irish missionary.

St Buryan's Church, St Buryan – Named after St Buriana, an Irish missionary and daughter of a Irish king.

Madron – Named after St Medrhan, an Irish missionary also known as St Maternus.

From the sixth century though to the fifteenth century the parish churches were constructed in West Cornwall, and the map I had produced shows the locations and towns where the churches were built.

In plotting the locations of the parish churches, a similar pattern emerges to the location of the ancient settlements. While it is true that the parish churches are a little further inland, they are evenly distributed around the perimeter of the coastline almost in a watchtower formation. A number of the churches are in sight of each other and with the tower bells could provide early warning in the event of an invasion or attack. The invasion of Spanish forces in 1595 would have put this to the test when they burned the parish church in the village of Paul.

The short land bridge between the Lelant on the north coast and Perranthnoe on the south coast, was protected in ancient times by the Hill Forts of Trencrom Hill and Castle Pencair on Tregonning Hill. This eight-kilometre land line now has four parish churches situated on or nearby at Lelant, St Erth, St Hilary and Perranuthnoe. And from the parish church at Ludgvan there were views over this land strip and across Mount's Bay.

Several of these parish churches often had earlier chapels and places of worship on the site and as old as the present-day construction appears, it may not have been the first place of worship to have been built on the site.

The construction of a parish church is a costly undertaking requiring funding and detailed organisation. The mining and preparation of the granite building blocks for the walls and towers, stone for the columns and large amounts of timber work would have required a large labour force to complete the construction. Sixteen parish churches in a relatively small land area indicates that the population must have had access to substantial funds. I think that it is unlikely that these were simple farming communities and adds to the evidence of an established mining industry.

Over the years these churches have gone through different degrees of restoration, but it is a testament to the quality of construction and durability of the dressed stone in the towers and walls, that the buildings have survived from the Middle Ages.

Another fact that we can see from the locations of the parish churches is that these early Cornish inhabitants lived above the lower coastline and away from the coast. Around the west of Mount's Bay, the parish church at Paul is above the present-day towns of Mousehole and Newlyn. The parish church at Gulval is inland and elevated from the shoreline to the east of Penzance. The west and north coast of the peninsula is naturally protected in large part by the cliffs, and the parish churches are all situated at elevation and high above sea level. At Sennen, where there is a natural sea cove, the parish church is situated inland and at elevation, and is within sight of St Buryan's church.

The names of the parish churches and the saints they were named after show the close ties to the Irish, English, French and Welsh missionaries that came to Cornwall, and in particular West Cornwall, around the fifth century. The construction of these parish churches starts from the sixth century, but really gathers pace in the thirteenth to fifteenth centuries, and in nearly all cases the parish church was named centuries after the patron saint had passed away.

The churches are all Grade II listed buildings and are in the database of Historic England. The listing often includes features nearby to the church, such as walls and crosses.

St Creden Parish Church, Sancreed

The church is named for St Sancredus with variations on the name including St Creden, St Credus, St Credanus and St Sancres. The Cornish word for Sancreed is 'Eglossancres'.

I visited Sancreed Parish Church as part of a joint visit to Sancreed Beacon and was happy to find it open, with helpful guide notes for visitors. Parts of the church date back to the thirteenth, fourteenth and fifteenth centuries, and the building was restored in the nineteenth century, and again in the early twentieth century. It is believed that an earlier place of worship existed in the church location from before the Norman Conquest, which I thought seemed highly likely given the arrival of the early missionaries in the fifth century and the nearby location of a holy well. I learned from the church visitor information that in 2017, after a period of fundraising, the church was restored with amongst others, a new roof and lead flashings. In the silence of the building I thought on its importance as a place of Christian worship, and that it was the centre of the community in years past, celebrating joyful occasions such as christenings and marriages.

Stanhope Alexander Forbes (1857 – 1947) who was considered the father of the Newlyn School of artists, was a regular attender at the church, and is buried in the church grounds.

The Methodist minister John Wesley attended a church service at St Creden on Sunday, September 4, 1768, where he noted in his diary that he heard an 'excellent' sermon. This was John Wesley's second visit to Sancreed as he had preached outside of the church six years earlier on September 12, 1762. When I visited St Creden I had that singular thought that if walls could talk, what a tale they could tell of the people who went in and out of their doors over the hundreds and hundreds of years.

St Buryan's Church, St Buryan

St Buryan is situated on southern central side of the Land's End and Penwith Peninsula. From the tower at St Buryan's church, the parish church at Sennen on the western side of the peninsula is in sight. John Wesley preached outside of the church on two occasions, the first on Sunday, September 7, 1766, and the second on Sunday, August 25, 1782. On both occasions he had preached in the nearby village of Mousehole in the morning, before riding to St Buryan and speaking after the Sunday church service had finished.

The current tower dates from the sixteenth century, but a church has been on this site since the tenth century, and the church records indicate that an oratory may have been on the site centuries before that. The church was dedicated in 1238 and further restoration work took place in the sixteenth century. The church was named for St Buriana, a holy woman who came from Ireland in the sixth century and who was said to be the daughter of an Irish king. This is the parish that King Athelstan visited on his tenth-century campaign in Cornwall, and is reported to have stayed overnight. St Buryan is one of the largest parish churches on the Land's End and Penwith Peninsula and was undergoing further restoration work when I visited in 2019 and 2020.

St Levan Church, St Levan

Located on the southern part of the Land's End and Penwith Peninsula, the church is a few miles to the west of the Minack Theatre and Porthcurnoe Beach. Although this is now quite a remote area, in John Norden's Topographical And Historical Description of Cornwall *(1728)*, he notes, 'Near unto, and within this parishe are manie Tynn mynes'. He also described the little cove with its fishing boats.

A church has existed on this site since medieval times and was substantially rebuilt in the thirteenth and fifteenth centuries. When I visited in 2019 St Levan Parish Church was undergoing major renovations.

The parish church name of St Leven comes from the Celtic form of Solomon, which has variants of Selevan and Saloman. The name St Levan is the name given to James and Mary St Aubyn (Lord and Lady St Levan), who reside on St Michael's Mount.

St Sennen's Church, Sennen

Sennen is located on the west coast of the peninsula just to the north of Land's End. The western section of the Cornwall coastal path links Land's End to Sennen Cove and passes by the ancient site of Castle Maen.

A sign at the front of Sennen Parish Church gives a date for the building of AD 520. However, further work took place at later dates and the church font dates back to the fourteenth century or possibly earlier. The church is dedicated to St Sinnius also known as St Senan and St Senanus, believed to be a sixth century Irish Bishop. The site is one of the oldest sites of Christian worship in West Cornwall.

John and Charles Wesley visited Sennen on separate occasions, and John Wesley preached there on Saturday, September 10, 1743. Both men used the visit as an opportunity to visit nearby Land's End and climb down the rocks as far as they could. After the Wesley brothers' visit to nearby Land's End, a particular rock formation became known as the Wesley Stone. It was claimed that John Wesley wrote part of a hymn at this location:

> *Lo! on a narrow neck of land,*
> *'Twixt two unbounded seas I stand,*
> *Secure insensible:*
> *A point of life, a moment's space . . .*

For many years postcards were sold of John Wesley and the Land's End 'Wesley Rock'.

Sennen was the location of a historical event during the reign of King Henry VII. Perkin Warbeck (1474 – 1499) had claimed to be Richard, Duke of York and the second son of King Edward IV, and had tried several times to assert his claim to the throne without success. On September 7, 1497 he sailed into Sennen Cove with the intention of raising an army against King Henry VII.

The Cornish had been involved in an uprising that same year against war taxes imposed by King Henry VII, and, together with other forces that joined en route, made it to London. The King's forces attacked the uprising in what was known as the Battle of Deptford Bridge and the uprising was crushed. The leaders of the Cornish, Michael Joseph (known as Michael An Gof – Michael the blacksmith) and Thomas Flamank, were captured and executed at Tyburn on June 27, 1497. A commemorative plaque was placed in Blackheath Common and a statue was erected in St Keverne as a memorial to the uprising. Capitalising on the emotions caused by the failure of the uprising, Perkin Warbeck was able to rally an army of some six thousand men. He was declared as Richard IV on Bodmin Moor and led his forces first to Exeter, and then on to Taunton in Somerset. On hearing that the King had sent his chief general and that forces were closing in, Perkin Warbeck deserted his army and was later captured in Hampshire. The leaders of the army with Perkin Warbeck were rounded up and executed, others were fined, and the force returned to Cornwall. Perkin Warbeck was given some latitude by King Henry VII after he confessed to being an imposter; however, he was later executed at Tyburn in 1499.

St Pol de Leon's Church, Paul

The village of Paul is above the harbour town of Mousehole and is the parish church for both communities. The church tower is visible from a number of locations within Mount's Bay and from the church tower in Ludgvan, several miles away.

Founded in AD 490 by Paul Aurelian, a Welsh saint, the church was largely destroyed by the Spanish during their invasion of 1595. Over the next five years funds were collected to allow the church to be rebuilt by 1600.

Within the churchyard and inset into the church perimeter wall there is a monument dedicated to Dolly Portreath, reputed to have been the last speaker of the ancient Cornish language. Dolly Portreath died in 1777 and her memorial stone was erected by Prince Louis Lucien Bonaparte and the Reverend John Garret, Vicar of St Paul, in 1860. Prince Lucien Bonaparte was the nephew of Napoleon Bonaparte who had died just 39 years earlier. Prince Lucien had made a detailed study of languages, including a study of English dialects, which explained his interest in Dolly Portreath.

The memorial stone is inscribed:

HONOUR THY FATHER AND THY MOTHER

THAT THY DAYS MAY BE LONG UPON

THE LAND THAT THE LORD THY GOD

GIVETH THEE.   EXOD XX.12

GWRA PERTHI DE TAX HE DE MAM

MAL DE DYTHIOW BETHENZ HYR WAR

AN TYR NEB AN ARLETH DE DEW.

BYES DEES.   EXOD XX.12

In 1860, when the memorial stone was erected, Napoleon III (born Charles-Louis Napoleon Bonaparte) was the reigning monarch of France. He was the last King of France and reigned until September 4, 1870, when the French lost the battle of Sedan to the Prussians and he was taken as a prisoner of war. Eventually released, Napoleon III was transferred to Camden House in Chislehurst, Kent, where he lived out the last few years of his life from 1871–1873.

The Cornish language had been on the decline since the introduction of the Book of Common Prayer in 1549, and the Act of Uniformity passed in 1549 made it law that all Parish Churches follow the new book. This new law led to a rebellion in Cornwall, driven by the fact that the book was in English, as well as an objection to the changes themselves. The rebellion spread and it is believed that over five thousand people lost their lives. Proposals to translate the Book of Common Prayer into Cornish were rejected, and in the two hundred years following 1549, the native Cornish language died out.

St Just Parish Church, St Just in Penwith

Located to the north of the Land's End and Penwith Peninsula, St Just was the largest mining town in the area. The Parish Church was dedicated to St Just in 1478, and is the only parish church in the north-west peninsula.

The current building dates from the fifteenth century, but there have been earlier churches on the site at least back to the fourteenth century.

The Selus Stone is within the parish church and is thought to date to the fifth century. It has a Latin inscription meaning Selus lies here. A possible reference to Saloman of Cornwall or St Seleven, which translates to St Levan.

The church grounds were used by John Wesley when he visited Cornwall and St Just to preach. He usually stayed overnight in St Just and enjoyed some of his largest congregations when he spoke there. It was here on Tuesday, July 2, 1745 that a warrant of arrest, issued by Dr Borlase, was served on John Wesley. The arrest warrant came to nothing and John Wesley continued his visits over many years; his final visit to St Just was on Thursday, August 20, 1789, at the age of eighty-six.

Charles Wesley also visited St Just on several occasions, he preached on Saturday, July 20, 1743 and attended the evening service in the Church the following day.

St Senara's Church, Zennor

Located on the north coast of the Land's End and Penwith Peninsula, the Parish Church in Zennor is located between the towns of St Ives and Morvah.

The Church is named after St Senara, a Cornish Saint and a Church has stood on this site since the sixth century. The present church dates to the twelth to fifteenth Centuries.

St Bridget's Church, Morvah

The church is thought to be dedicated to Swedish St Bridget who was canonised in 1391. However, an alternative theory is that the church is named after a sixth century Irish saint named Brigid of Kildare, who is one of the patron saints in Ireland. Given the Irish connection, with all of the surrounding parish churches, it seems that Saint Brigid of Kildare would be the more likely origin of the church name.

The tower is the only medieval part of the church dating back to 1400, the rest of the church is fifteenth century or later.

St Tewennocus, Towednack

Towednack is located between Zennor and St Ives just south of the B3306. The population was three hundred and fifty-seven in 2011 (including three other nearby hamlets) and even back in the 1700s it seems that Towednack was not much larger.

The church was built in the thirteenth century and extended in the fifteenth century with a south aisle. The base of the font is believed to be from the Norman period.

The church is believed to be dedicated to St Winwaloe (alternate Winnoc – Tewennocus) and therefore linked to the church at Gunwalloe.

Charles Wesley attended the Sunday church service at St Tewennocus Parish Church on July 17, 1743, where the Rev William Hoblyn was presiding. The Rev William Hoblyn and the Rev William Symonds worked with each other in the St Ives parish and were against the Methodist movement, and openly spoke out against Methodists and the Wesley brothers. After the service Charles Wesley spoke outside the church and it seems later had an altercation with the Rev Hoblyn. The following Sunday Charles Wesley returned and preached in the afternoon and later attended the evening service. Here it seems things took a nasty turn as a mob formed and tried to attack Chares Wesley. In his journal Charles Wesley described how he saw ten ruffians set upon one unarmed man, beating him with their clubs. With help from others, Charles Wesley managed to return to St Ives, with the mob still in pursuit. The following day Charles Wesley recorded in his journal: 'The Mayor told us, that the Ministers were the authors of all this evil, by continually representing us in their sermons as Popish emissaries, and urging the enraged multitude to take all manner of ways to stop us.'

St Tewennocus, Towednack featured as a film location in the 1975 series of Poldark.

St Uny Church, Lelant

Lelant is on the opposite side of the estuary from the town of Hayle and was once an important harbour. St Uny Church is situated close to the estuary and there are views out to sea looking north from the church grounds.

Parts of the original church dates back to 1100 when a Norman from Ludgvan Leaze built a stone church and separate tower. The church was extended in 1390 when two new aisles and the tower were built. Within the church is a beautiful stained-glass window showing St Uny, St Anta, St Ia, St Erth, St Winwaloe and St Gwinear.

St Uny interchanged with the spelling 'Euny' is also the patron saint of St Eny's Church in Redruth, and he was the brother of St Ia, the patron saint of St Ives. St Uny and St Ia landed at Lelant harbour around AD 600. The St Michael's Way, which crosses from the north to the south coast, starts at the church.

St Ia's Church, St Ives

St Ives is one of Cornwall's most popular tourist destinations and has visitors all year round. The town and the Parish Church take their name from St Ia, an Irish Princess who came to Cornwall as a missionary in the sixth century. St Ia was the sister of St Uny, St Anta and St Erca, all of whom have churches named after them in nearby Lelant, Carbis Bay and St Erth.

According to Dr William Borlase (1696 – 1772) in his book *Observations on the antiquities historical and monumental, of the county of Cornwall*, he records that St Ia and a number of other missionaries were put to death at Hayle estuary by King Tewdar.

The Parish Church is just a few yards above the harbour, and was built in the fifteenth century. This was not the first place of worship on this site as there was an earlier building, which is said to have been the burial place of St Ia.

The late Dame Barbara Hepworth, artist and sculptor, lived in St Ives from 1949 until her death in 1975. She created and donated a sculpture called the 'Madonna With Child' to St Ia's Church, which is permanently on display.

Gulval Church, Gulval

Gulval is located just north of the A30 as it passes between Long Rock and Penzance. Prior to the main road being constructed, Gulval would have been a passing point for travellers going to and from Penzance, connecting the nearby villages of Ludgvan and Varfell. The parish is believed to have been named after an Irish saint although the name of the saint would appear to have changed over time from its original.

The church in Gulval was built in the twelfth century with the tower added in the fifteenth century.

Both Charles Wesley and John Wesley preached in Gulval and on my visit to the Parish Church I was surprised to see an old banner from the Methodist Church. I was told that the banner was from the former Methodist church in Gulval, and on researching further I could see that the Methodists now meet in Gulval village hall. The old Methodist church in Gulval is now a grade II listed building, and its construction dates back to 1884.

St Paul Parish Church, Ludgvan

Ludgvan is located on a hill above Mount's Bay and commands views to St Michael's Mount in the south and to Tregonning Hill and Godolphin Hill to its east. Ludgvan has been a residential area for many centuries and is recorded in the Domesday Book, compiled in 1086. The church at Ludgvan can be viewed from the top of Penzance High Street and many locations around Mount's Bay. It would have been a significant look out location for activity in the area.

The Church of England website notes that there has been a place of worship on the site of the present church since the seventh century, and that this was originally dedicated to St Ludewon, with alternate spelling of Ludvon. The present church dates back to the fourteenth century and was dedicated to St. Paul on July 14, 1336. The impressive church tower followed in the fifteenth century

Inside the church there is a memorial to William Borlase the antiquarian who was also the Rector of the Church between 1722 and 1772, and also to the parents of Sir Humphrey Davy (1778 – 1829). The Davy family worked a farm in nearby Varfell, and would have been regular attendees. The church font dates from the Norman period.

St Piran's and St Michael's Parish Church, Perranuthnoe

Located to the east of St Michael's Mount and Marazion, Pernanuthnoe is a coastal town above a large sandy beach. The southern part of the Cornish coastal footpath between Prussia Cove and Marazion passes around the peninsula at Pernanuthnoe.

The church is dedicated to St Piran, a fifth century Cornish Abbot of Irish descent and St Michael. St Piran is generally adopted as the patron saint of Cornwall and St Piran's flag is the flag of Cornwall, with a white cross on a black background.

Perranuthnoe was recorded in the Domesday Book of 1086 as Odenaol. The name changed over time becoming Udno and the Uthnoe-veor in the nineteenth century. The addition of Piran or Perran completes the modern-day name Perranuthnoe.

St Erth's Church, St Erth

A fourteenth century church that was dedicated to St Erc, an Irish saint, who went on a mission to Cornwall centuries earlier. The church was restored in the eighteenth and nineteenth centuries, although the tower remains as part of the original building.

St Maddern's Church, Madron

The Parish Church in Madron is named after Saint Madron (alternative St Maddern) who was a of Cornish descent and lived in the sixth century. The church was built much later and the structure dates to the fourteen and fifteenth century. Dr Walter Borlase (1694 – 1776), the brother of Dr William Borlase, was the rector of St Maddern's as well as St Bridget's Parish Church in Morvah.

Madron Well and Madron Well Chapel are located north of the town of Madron. Madron well was considered to be a holy well.

PARISH CHURCHES – TO THE EAST OF THE LAND'S END AND PENWITH PENINSULA

St Breage's Church, Breage

Breage is located just west of Helston and near to Godolphin Cross and Tregonning Hill.

A fifteenth century church dedicated to Saint Breague or Breaca, an Irish missionary nun who came to Cornwall in the fifth century.

This church was the nearest parish church to the Godolphin Estate and the Godolphin family records show baptisms and marriages in the church.

St Felicitas and St Piala's Church, Phillack, Hayle

St Felicitas and St Piala's Church, Phillack is a church dating from the twelfth century, with a fifteenth century tower. Located above the Hayle estuary, the church would have been an important stopping point for Christian pilgrims coming from Ireland, Wales and the north of England. The church underwent major reconstruction in the mid-nineteenth century.

The church is dedicated to Saint Felicitas (alternate Felec or Felix) a British Saint in Cornwall during the sixth century. Saint Piala is believed to be the sister of Saint Gwinear.

Phillack is to the north of Hayle and to the south of Hayle is the village of Gwinear. Settlers to Australia must have come from this area as there is a Mt St Phillack and Mt St Gwinear in Baw Baw National Park, Victoria, Australia, about forty kilometres east of Melbourne. These two mountains are separated by less than two miles – a similar distance between the Parish Church in Phillack and the Parish Church in Gwinear.

St Gwinear's Church, Gwinear

This parish church dates from the thirteenth and fourteenth century, with the tower erected in the fifteenth century. The church was renovated before the end of the nineteenth century. The church is dedicated to St Winierus, also known as St Gwinear, the leader of the Irish missionaries who came to Cornwall in the 6th century.

The churches were constructed and renovated over different time periods and different styles of architecture. The later church towers follow the Norman style of architecture.

St Gothian's Church, Gwithian

This parish church was built in the thirteenth century and the tower added in the fifteenth century. As with St Gwinear's Church and St Felicitas, the church underwent extensive rebuilding in the nineteenth century.

The Church of St Hilary, St Hilary

This church has a thirteenth century tower and is dedicated to Saint Hilary of Poitiers.

IN THE FOOTSTEPS OF JOHN WESLEY

LTHOUGH I TOOK MY CUE for researching the journals of John Wesley when he was in West Cornwall from my visit to Tregonning Hill, I have come to realise that any review of Cornish history would not be complete without reference to his visits and work in Cornwall between 1743, and the end of his life in 1791. During this period John Wesley visited Cornwall over thirty times and while he did not claim to have founded the Methodist movement, he is associated with Methodism, and often accredited as its founder. The historical buildings that can still be seen in towns and villages of West Cornwall from the late-seventeen-hundreds until the late-eighteen-hundreds are the Methodist and Wesleyan churches. There is hardly a town or village in Cornwall without a Methodist or Wesleyan church. It was reported that by the late-eighteen-hundreds, ninety percent of the population in Cornwall were Methodists.

Many of these Methodist and Wesleyan churches can still be seen today and most have a date engraved on a stone, that identifies the year they were constructed. Interestingly, most of the churches were built fifty to one hundred years after the death of John Wesley, and this perhaps reflected the growth of Methodism after his passing, and an improvement in the economy during the boom in mining from the mid-eighteen-hundreds.

The construction of many of these churches was to very high standards using local granite and stone, and for this reason they have stood the test of time.

In Cornwall's application to UNESCO for listing as a World Heritage Site, the work of John Wesley is acknowledged as a pioneer of Methodism and the application notes that over seven hundred chapels exist in Cornwall and eighty-percent of them are Methodist.

John Wesley was born on June 28, 1703, in Epworth, Lincolnshire. His parents were Samuel and Susanna Wesley and he had ten surviving siblings out of the nineteen children born to his parents. His mother had taken it upon herself to educate and teach her children and did this very successfully. In addition to an educational curriculum, Susanna Wesley imparted her values and beliefs on the children and spent time with each child individually during the week. During their formative years, the children learned to plan and use their time wisely and were led by the example of their mother who divided her day into set activities and prioritised time for prayer and study. Learning from his parents, John Wesley grew with similar values and throughout his life maintained a discipline in how he lived his life and used his time.

After spending his childhood in Lincolnshire, he left to study and board at Charterhouse School and later at Christ Church College, Oxford. In 1726, he was elected a Fellow of Lincoln College, Oxford.

John Wesley was part of a group at Oxford called the Holy Club, and was disciplined and devout in his religious belief. He had at this point in his life already decided that he wanted to be an ordained minister, following in his father's footsteps.

By 1728 John Wesley was an ordained Anglican minister and he remained part of the Church of England.

John Wesley was based in Oxford for some years and later spent two years in America as a minister in Savannah, which was part of the relatively new Georgia province. After deciding to return to England, he set sail on Christmas Eve, December 24, 1737, and records in his journal that they sailed close to the Isles of Scilly on January 28, 1738. From there the ship sailed past the Lizard point, the most southerly part in Britain, on Sunday, January 29.

On Wednesday May 24, 1738, John Wesley describes having gone unwillingly to a religious meeting in Aldersgate Street, London. During that service John Wesley described his heart as 'being strangely warmed'. This day was certainly a turning point for John Wesley and marked an important milestone in his ministry, which became known at Methodism or Wesleyanism.

George Whitfield was an evangelist whom John Wesley had met in Oxford when they studied together. Like Wesley, Whitfield had also ministered in Savanah, Georgia Province, America and the two ministers had remained in contact. On Saturday, March 31, 1739, John Wesley travelled to Bristol to meet George Whitfield, who had taken to preaching to crowds in the open air. John Wesley records how 'I could scarcely reconcile myself at first to this strange way of preaching in the fields'. On Sunday, April 1, 1739, George Whitfield had departed, and John Wesley preached for the first time in the open air.

Now in his mid-thirties, John Wesley started to travel and preach throughout Britain and also visited Ireland on numerous occasions.

John Wesley's first visit to Cornwall was in 1743. The reception he received in Cornwall and other places was often hostile and on many occasions John Wesley found himself confronted by an angry mob. The local church ministers were not in favour of the Wesley brothers, or their outdoor preaching. In many places the local ministers stirred up their parishioners against the Wesleys, considering them a threat, and certainly not conforming to established church practice.

To give a picture of the religious landscape at the time, it would be fair to say that the Church of England exerted far more control then than it does now. Some eighty years earlier the Conventicle Act of 1664 came into force and this banned religious gatherings of five or more people outside of the established Church of England.

On August 14, 1670, William Penn, who went on to be the founder of Pennsylvania, America and William Mead were arrested and charged with preaching to an unlawful assembly in Grace Church Street, London. The jury returned a verdict saying that the two men were guilty of speaking in Grace Church Street, but refused to add 'to an unlawful assembly'. The Judge, Justice Howell, was so angered by the verdict and threatened the jury by saying: 'Gentlemen; you shall not be dismissed till we have a verdict that the court will accept; and you shall be locked up without meat, drink, fire, and tobacco; you shall not think thus to abuse the court.' The plight of the jury became a separate case known as Bushel's case, named after the head juror Edward Bushel. This case went on to set a precedent that juries could not be threatened or intimidated into making a decision. A plaque marking the case can be seen at the Old Bailey in London.

Tensions were also high in parts of Cornwall and in April 1729, St Ives witnessed a riot led by 'tinners' from nearby Redruth. The people of St Ives requested additional military resources to be sent to Redruth to monitor and control the rioters and prevent any further disturbances. The situation was diffused by the riot ringleaders, led by Andrew Harris, who wrote to the Mayor of St Ives asking for clemency, and promising that there would be no repeat of the trouble.

Within Cornwall, and as part of their plan to disrupt the message John Wesley was teaching, the local ministers and authorities incited crowds against him. It was a pattern repeated in other parts of the country. In Cornwall during John Wesley's early visits, rumours were spread that he was involved in leading an uprising. On a visit to Towednack Parish Church on Sunday, July 24, 1743 Charles Wesley was the subject of a violent mob's attention and on Thursday, July 4, 1745, John Wesley was attacked by a mob in Falmouth.

Undeterred, John Wesley continued his ministry in Cornwall and over time the atmosphere changed, and many people converted to Methodism. Their impact on the county and on its history was immense.

Charles Wesley was also a visitor to Cornwall in 1743 and returned for several other visits. He and John Wesley would on occasion attend St Euny church near Redruth for services, as well as other Parish Churches throughout the area. Charles Wesley also preached outdoors at Kennegy Downs near Tregonning Hill.

John Wesley kept a journal from October 1735 until October 1790. Extracts from these journals give us a detailed account of his travels. He was often on the move and it is estimated that in a peak year he had travelled eight thousand miles. In Cornwall he went from place to place, normally preaching outside to crowds that were estimated to have reached thirty thousand in the latter stages of his ministry.

On Friday June 21, 1745, John Wesley visited St Michael's Mount to attend a judicial hearing for a Methodist minister, Mr Maxfield. The local magistrates had ordered the arrest of Mr Maxfield to stop him preaching and leading a local church, primarily because he was not an ordained minister. The expected punishment for this offence was to be press ganged into the navy or sent to the army. The warrant had been signed by the steward of John St Aubyn, and in attendance at the hearing was Dr Borlase, a magistrate and local rector. John Wesley was asked why he was at the hearing, and having explained, was then asked to wait until the case came up later that day. He was never called, and on further enquiry found out the case had been heard and that Mr Maxfield had been dispatched to the dungeon in Penzance. John Wesley made a note in his journal about the visit and commented, 'The house at the top is surprisingly large and pleasant. Sir John St Aubyn had taken much pains and been at considerable expense in repairing and beautifying the apartments; and when the seat was finished, the owner died.' This was a reference to Sir John St Aubyn, 3rd Baronet (1695 – 1744) who had passed away the year before John Wesley's visit.

In 1745, John Wesley and a small group sailed from St Ives harbour to the Isles of Scilly. They arrived at St Mary's at one thirty in the afternoon on Tuesday, September 13, and straight away went to see the governor of the island, with the customary gift of a newspaper from the mainland. Francis Godolphin, Second Earl of Godolphin, had been appointed Governor of the Isles of Scilly following the death of his father and followed a long line of Godolphins overseeing the Isles of Scilly. One point of conversation might have been a common thread with St Paul's Cathedral. John Wesley's grandfather, the Rev Samuel Annesley (1620 -1696), had been the lecturer at St Paul's Cathedral in 1657, and was appointed by Oliver Cromwell to the position. This was before the return of King Charles II and the great fire of London in 1666, which partly destroyed the Cathedral and led to its subsequent rebuilding. Henry Godolphin, brother to Sidney, First Earl of Godolphin and uncle of Francis Godolphin, Second Earl of Godolphin, had been the Dean of St Paul's Cathedral from July 14, 1707, until 1726. Henry Godolphin had actually been connected with St Paul's since November 1683 at a time it was being rebuilt to the design of Sir Christopher Wren.

John Wesley and the Methodists set up a system of support for those in need and established timetables and locations, known as circuits, for ministers to preach to their congregations in different towns. These smaller groups were known as societies, and each society would be responsible for a village, town or even larger area. During John Wesley's visits to Cornwall, he would often preach at a venue he had preached at before, at the same of the year, and at the same time of the day. John Wesley lived a simple exemplary life of service, he spurned the comforts of his residence in London for months on the road, witnessing to congregations of God's grace. Not only did this give the people of Cornwall spiritual hope, he ensured that the Methodist movement provided practical help for those families caught in poverty and despair. For families reliant on income from mining there were times of want and times of plenty. When mines closed or production slowed, unemployment was rife, and families were left in extreme poverty with no social support system to help them. It is clear from the reaction to John Wesley's visits that he brought a message of hope and change that was to have a great impact on those who heard him.

Dr William Borlase was the rector of Ludgvan Church from 1722 and not kindly disposed to untrained Methodist ministers and his brother, Dr Walter Borlase, was the rector at the nearby Madron Parish Church. Neither of them seemed to know much about John Wesley, other than he was a preacher involved with the Methodist movement. On Tuesday, July 2, 1745, Dr Borlase issued a warrant for John Wesley's arrest, which was served by Mr Eustick in St Just, after John Wesley had preached there. Some reports have William Borlase issuing the warrant and others have Walter Borlase; John Wesley's own journal of the incident simply refers to Dr Borlase, which does not help identify which brother he is referring to. Also, there are two Mr Ustickes, Mr. William Usticke Justice of Peace, is mentioned in the edited footnotes of John Wesley's journal for an incident that happened a week earlier, and other reports have a Mr Stephen Usticke, who was the brother-in-law of the Borlase brothers, being married to their sister Catherine. John Wesley and Mr Usticke rode a few miles south the next day only to find Dr Borlase out. Mr Usticke, claiming he had fulfilled his duty, rode off, and John Wesley headed back to his base in St Ives. There must have been a realisation at this time or shortly after, that John Wesley was an ordained minister. The arrest warrant never came up again and John Wesley preached several times in Ludgvan outside of the Parish Church, where Dr William Borlase was rector. It seems that at this point that both brothers also eased up on his persecution of Methodist ministers. Mr Stephen Usticke died the following year aged forty-six.

A connection between an ancestor of John Wesley and King Charles II occurred after the Battle of Worcester in 1651. This battle had taken place after Prince Charles returned from the continent and was crowned King of Scotland. With the Scottish forces behind him, he marched into England as far as Worcester and stopped there. Within days the parliamentarian forces led by Oliver Cromwell surrounded the city, and after a short wait they attacked the King's forces held up in Worcester. The royalists lost the battle, and their forces scattered with many attempting to head north back to Scotland. King Charles went on the run, disguised himself and hid in various locations – initially travelling north and then heading south through Warwickshire, Gloucestershire, Somerset and Dorset. One of the hiding locations was in an oak tree at Boscobel

House in Staffordshire and this is where we have the name Royal Oak. When in Dorset looking for a ship to bring him to the continent, King Charles and his small party passed through the village of Charmouth and stayed at an inn. As they were leaving they discovered that one of the horses needed a shoe repaired. They went to the village blacksmith, who, while checking the other horses recognised a Worcester marking on a shoe. There was a reward on offer for information leading to the arrest of King Charles of one-thousand-pounds, an absolute fortune at that time. The party left and the blacksmith immediately went to see the local Vicar to report this. The Rev B. Westley took the report and immediately sent the information on to the parliamentarian military force in nearby Lyme Regis. The King evaded capture and subsequently made his escape to France. After Oliver Cromwell died, he was invited back to take the Monarchy. Following the King's coronation in 1661, he hunted down all who had signed his father's death warrant, and rewarded all those who had helped him, including the Godolphin family. The Rev B. Westley was removed as Rector of Charmouth in 1662 in a move that appeared to stem from his attempt to have the king captured on his escape from Worcester. The Rev B. Westley was the great grandfather of John and Charles Wesley.

Another coincidence occurred between John Wesley and the grandson of King James II, the brother of King Charles II. King Charles had fathered twelve children with a number of mistresses, but they were considered illegitimate, and were not in line to the throne. On the death of King Charles II, the crown passed to his brother James (1633 – 1701) who became King James II. The reign of King James II only lasted three years and he was deposed in 1688. It was again a question of religion; James had converted to Catholicism in a secret ceremony in 1668, which was no longer a secret. On the birth of his second son in 1688, there was concern that the crown would move away from his daughter Mary, born to his first protestant wife Ann. Mary, who had been brought up an Anglican, had married William of Orange, a staunch protestant. With the crown lost, William and Mary reigned as sovereign and James went into exile. The Stuart family had not given up hope of reclaiming the throne, and the son of the deposed King James II, Francis Edward Stuart (1688 – 1766) also known as the Old Pretender, led a Jacobite rising in 1715 in an attempt to reclaim the throne. The Jacobites supported a return of the throne to King James II and his successors.

The Old Pretender did not succeed in reclaiming the throne despite several uprisings. When he died, his son, Charles Edward Stuart (1720 – 1788) took up the cause and was known as The Young Pretender, and later as Bonnie Prince Charlie. The Young Pretender had threatened to return to Britain and lead an uprising, which posed a serious and credible threat to the Monarchy.

It is here an interesting connection occurs that takes us back to Cornwall and John Wesley. John Wesley had started his visits to Cornwall in September 1743, and he had used the harbour town of St Ives as his base. In 1743 John Wesley had travelled into Cornwall with a small group consisting of the Rev W Shepherd, Mr John Nelson and Mr John Downes. The group stayed three weeks in Cornwall before travelling east and back into Devon. In 1744, John Wesley returned to Cornwall again and recorded in his journal that Wednesday, April 11, was a public fast and that he attended a church service at St Ia's Parish Church in St Ives. The public fast had been ordered on the occasion of the threatened invasion by the Young Pretender. Two weeks later, and on his way back out of Cornwall, John Wesley stopped with Digory and Elizabeth Isbel at their house in Trewint, on the east side of Bodmin Moor, near Altarnun. It was here Digory Isbel informed John Wesley of an accusation against him that had been travelling around the county.

John Wesley had already heard the accusation that he had brought the Young Pretender to Cornwall on his autumn visit the year before, under the name of John Downes. This updated accusation was that he called himself John Wesley, whereas everyone knew Mr Wesley was dead. The rumour persisted and on John Wesley's visit the following year he had a confrontation with officials. It was on Thursday, July 4, 1745, while John Wesley was riding in Wendron parish, following a visit to Falmouth, that a group of Church Wardens, Constables and the heads of the parish were waiting to intercept him. One of the party informed John Wesley: 'Sir, I will tell you the ground of this. All the gentlemen on these parts say that you have been a long time in France and are now sent hither by the Pretender; and these societies are to join him.' By societies he meant the newly formed Methodist Societies that were being established in different locations around the county and the country.

It was just a few weeks later, on July 23, 1745, that the Young Pretender landed in Scotland looking to lead an uprising. As with all such uprisings rumours abounded about what might happen and when, and this was answered when the rebellion began in the Scottish Highlands in August 1745. By September the Jacobites and forces loyal to Charles Stuart had captured Edinburgh and had beat English forces in the Battle of Prestonpans. In October of the same year the Scots agreed to invade England, with Charles promising support from the French, who would invade southern England, and English Jacobites who would rally to the cause.

The Scottish army led by Charles was referred to as the Jacobites and they crossed into England in November, and by December had reached Derby. With little support from English Jacobites and no sign of the French, the army assessed that they would be outnumbered in any conflict and decided to return to Scotland, much to the dismay of Charles.

The English forces pursued the Jacobites into Scotland and the sides clashed in Falkirk on January 1746. The English were defeated on the day but regrouped by April when the sides met in the Battle of Culloden. This battle was a comprehensive defeat for Charles Stuart and the Jacobite forces. Charles had to escape and spent months in disguise looking for a way back to France. Unable to rally support for a further attempt to claim the throne, Charles died in Rome in 1788.

The visits of John Wesley continued over many years and he had a genuine affection for West Cornwall. He would in his early years spend more time in this area than any other part of Cornwall, using St Ives as his base. From his journal we have records of multiple visits to Helston, Marazion, Penzance, Gulval, Mousehole and Newlyn on the south coast, and multiple visits to St Just, Morvah, Zennor and Lelant on the north coast. In his later years thousands would turn out to see him, perhaps knowing it could be for the last time when he was in his eighties. In places where he had been attacked and had met with violence in years past, he was now venerated and received with joy. While he visited many locations in West Cornwall, including villages such as Goldsithney, St Hillary, Sancreed and many others, from the beginning of his journeys until the end he would not neglect visiting and preaching in St Ives and St Just.

One observer remarked of John Wesley's visits in later life: 'When he was last in the county Wesley passed through the towns and villages as in a triumphal march, whilst the windows were crowded with people anxious to get a sight of him and to pronounce upon him their better directions; yet he says not a word of it all.' Fittingly we do hear from John Wesley about his visit to Falmouth on Tuesday, August 17, 1789. Now at the age of eighty-six and on his last tour of Cornwall he wrote, 'The last time I was here, about forty years ago, I was taken prisoner by an immense mob, gaping and roaring like lions. But how is the tide turned! High and low now lined the street, from one end of the town to the other, out of stark love and kindness, gaping and staring as if the King were going by. In the evening I preached on the smooth top of the hill, at a small distance from the sea, to the largest congregation I have ever seen in Cornwall, except in or near Redruth.'

A view of the Crowns, Botallack

St Michaels Mount

Dollar Cove

Lanyon Quoit

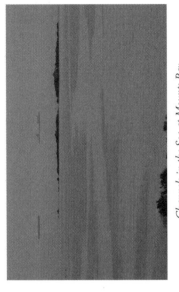

Men An Tol On The Land's End and Penwith Peninsula

Channels in the Sea at Mounts Bay

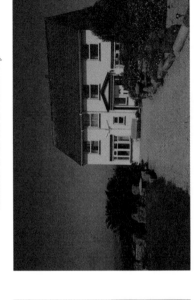

Tregonning Hill House

Clowance House, The Ancestral Home of the St Aubyn Family

The Strange Coloured Waters of a Cornish Clay Mine

Sancreed Parish Church – John Wesley Attended a
Service here on September 4, 1768

A Cornish Dry-Stone Wall Showing a Rich Contrast in Colours

The Merry Maidens Stone Circle

John Wesley 1703–1791

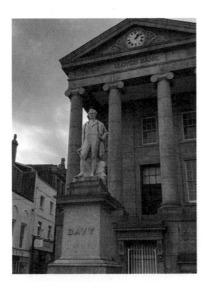

Sir Humphrey Davy Statue in Penzance, Erected in 1872.

Land's End, with the Longships Lighthouse in the Distance.

BOTALLACK MINE AND THE GOLDEN AGE OF MINING AND INNOVATION 1750-1900

ONE OF MY FAVOURITE PLACES TO VISIT is Botallack Mine on the North Coast of the Land's End and Penwith Peninsula, close to St Just. The property was purchased by the National Trust who own extensive tracks of land in the area. The area above the cliffs has many old engine houses and chimney stacks, but what makes Botallack so special is that the two mines perched right on the edge of a cliff, on a sharp incline from the cliff tops. Known as the Crowns Engine Houses, the mines are set against a seascape, which photographers have captured in storms, and at sunsets and sunrise. The artist James Clark Hook (1819 – 1907) painted a similar scene in his work 'From Under The Sea', which has three miners sitting in a small ore car on railway tracks that descend into the mouth of the mine. Crowns mines are accessible from a path that runs down the side of the cliff, and it is only when you are at the mine buildings you realise how narrow the cliff is that they sit upon, and the steepness of the sides all around them. Above the mines and on National Trust property is the count house and other buildings ancillary to the mining operations.

The mining of tin and copper was a major industry in West Cornwall and had been taking place over many centuries. Long before the technology existed to pump deep mines clear of ground and surface water, open cast mining and other forms of shallow mining were commonplace. At Wheal Vor near Breage and Tregonning Hill, evidence of surface mining is believed to date back to Roman Times. Evidence at the Iron Age village of Chysauster, on the Land's End and Penwith Peninsula, indicates that smelting of ore to separate the metal component was being undertaken during the late Iron Age. It is claimed that the famous Ding Dong mines, situated near to ancient landmarks such as Men an Tol and Lanyon Quoit, have been mined since prehistoric times.

However, very little is known about mining in West Cornwall during the Iron Age or Bronze Age. Perhaps this is not unsurprising given its high value and the desire of the traders to keep the location and trading a secret. There is anecdotal evidence that mining, and the trading of tin and copper, must have been taking place given the elaborate defence system of forts and castles built on the Land's End and Penwith Peninsula. If nothing of value existed, why go to such determined lengths to finance and build these impressive structures, which effectively turned the Peninsula into a fortress?

As we reach the Middle Ages and the advent of Christianity in West Cornwall, the question of how the construction of the Parish Churches was financed is a valid one. The population of the towns and villages where the parish churches were built was not substantial. How could these impressive structures have been paid for if there were not a valuable trade from mining?

It is reasonable to assume that tin and copper ore has been mined over thousands of years and the eighteenth and nineteenth century granite engine houses and chimney stacks that we can still see today, represent not only the peak of mining in Cornwall, but from an historical viewpoint they also marked the beginning of the end of this mining tradition.

Several parts of Cornwall and West Devon are registered as a World Heritage Site under UNESCO (United Nations Educational, Scientific and Cultural Organisation). Prince Charles was presented with the UNESCO certificate on May 10, 2007, at Cotehele House, Cornwall, and the description of the Cornwall World Heritage Site states:

Much of the landscape of Cornwall and West Devon was transformed in the 18th and early 19th centuries as a result of rapid growth of pioneering copper and tin mining. Its deep underground mines, engine houses, foundries, new towns, smallholdings, ports and harbours, and their ancillary industries together reflect prolific innovation which, in the early 19th century, enabled the region to produce two-thirds of the world's supply of copper. The substantial remains are a testimony to the contribution Cornwall and West Devon made to the industrial revolution in the rest of Britain and to the fundamental influence the area had on the mining world at large. Cornish technology embodied in engines, engine houses and mining equipment was exported around the world. Cornwall and West Devon were the heartland from which mining technology rapidly spread.

The term 'the Golden Age of Mining and Innovation 1750 – 1900' may be a misnomer, since the mining industry was active in Cornwall over several thousand years, and by most measures mining must have been profitable over the centuries in order to finance the development of the West Cornish communities. The measure of what constitutes a 'Golden Age' is also subjective and only applies if we consider certain aspects such as technological advancement, total mining output, financial investment and speculation.

Mining drove the development of machinery and steam driven pumps needed to keep the mines clear of water as the ore loads went deeper and deeper. The early steam pumps included the Savery Pump built in 1698 by Thomas Savery (1650 – 1715) and the Newcomen Engine, built in 1712 and designed by Thomas Newcomen (1664 – 1729). Later still, James Watt (1736 – 1819), a Scottish Engineer, brought further improvements to the steam engine in 1776. After teaming up with Mathew Boulton, the new firm Boulton and Watt successfully deployed their new engines to the Cornish mines and made a great financial success from their business venture. A few years later a Cornishman, Richard Trevithick (1771 – 1833) developed high pressure steam engines and had multiple designs, including steam engines for use in locomotives. Richard Trevithick was born in Tregajorran, near Illogan and Carn Brea, and grew up in the Redruth and Cambourne area. He also had first-hand mining experience and his father was a mine manager.

With the ability to mine deeper, the output of copper and tin peaked during the nineteenth century. During this period there were times of high demand and also times when demand dropped off and the price slumped.

The success of one mine drove the speculation and investment in multiple new ventures. The opportunity and potential to make a fortune led to a host of new mines being financed and built, which in turn drove the total output of mined ore and helped build the technological advances. For mine owners and investors, risk and rewards were there in good measure with some mine owners making incredible gains while many others lost their investments. The engine houses of the mines of this period were also solidly built from granite and this was a deliberate strategy to emphasise the potential quality of the mine and its prospects and to attract investors. As to the quality of construction, this can be testified to by the fact that they remain visible, even to the present day, across the Cornish countryside.

To understand a little more about mining at this time in history, it is helpful to separate tin and copper mining. Tin was an established mining tradition in Cornwall that became a regulated industry, and was administered by the stannaries. A stannary represented a mining district and the word stannary is from the Latin stannum (meaning tin). The chemical element symbol for tin is Sn, which comes from the word stannum. Within Cornwall there were four stannaries and these were located in Foweymore, Blackmore, Tywarnhaile and Penwith & Kernier.

The stannaries governed all aspects of tin mining, setting laws and enforcing them through its own courts. In return for these powers, the stannaries paid tax to the Crown, and in Cornwall, paid tax to the Duchy of Cornwall from 1338, after its creation as a Duchy in 1337 by King Edward III. The stannary of Penwith & Kernier covered the West Cornwall mining districts of Tregonning and St Just.

Within the stannary system ore from a mine would be sent to a licensed smelting company. Once smelted, the tin was cast into blocks or ingots that had the smelter's name marked on and a further mark to indicate the quality of the tin. From the smelter, the tin would travel to the coinage hall where a corner would be taken from the ingot to assess quality and the tax would be paid. There were strict rules about when ingots could be transported from the smelter to the coinage hall and what routes could be used. Once the tax was paid the coinage hall would stamp the block of tin and it would be then free for onward trading. In West Cornwall the coinage town was in Penzance and the nearest coinage town from Penzance was nearly thirty miles away in Truro. The Coinage Hall in Truro was in the heart of the city on Boscawen Street, and the present-day Coinage Hall sits on the site of the original building.

In contrast, copper mining was not covered by the stannary system and the copper ore was often transported out of the county for smelting. South Wales, near to the coalfields, was a common location for smelting and copper ore from Cornwall was sometimes sent there. Copper mines were, in general, far more profitable than tin mines and paid higher dividends. Often mines interchanged mining for copper and tin and this can be seen in two of the richest mines in Cornish history:

Wheal Vor

This mine was located in Carleen, near Breage and in the shadow of Tregonning Hill. From the fifteenth century until 1715 Wheal Vor was a copper mine and linked to the Godolphin family, with Godolphin House just a few miles away. The mine used modern techniques and equipment to improve efficiency as the technology became available. It is claimed that the mine was one of the first to use gunpowder to open up new seams underground; it also utilised the Savery Pump and later the Newcomen Pump. After 1715, the mine was closed for a period of time and when it was reopened as a tin mine. The geology of the area repeatedly uncovered tin ore at a deeper level than copper ore.

After reopening, and from the early eighteen-hundreds until the mid-eighteen-hundreds, Wheal Vor was one of the most productive and profitable tin mines in Cornwall. With a decline in tin prices around 1850, and increased competition from overseas tin imports, mining activities at Wheal Vor declined dramatically with minimal production, until the mine finally closed in the early 1900s.

Dulcoath

Dulcoath mine was located near Cambourne and also held claim to being one of the most profitable mines in all of Cornwall. From 1720 – 1787 it was a copper mine before closing for over ten years between 1788 – 1799. When it reopened again in 1799 it continued as a copper mine until 1832. From 1833 Dulcoath was a tin mine and continued mining tin until its final closure in 1920. The mine also utilised the technology of the era and had a Newcomen Steam Engine installed in 1775. The father of Richard Trevithick (also Richard Trevithick) worked at the Dulcoath mine and this is where his son, the future inventor and pioneer of high-pressure steam engines, would have seen earlier steam machinery at work.

Mining was not solely the domain of men during this period; women and children were also employed at the mines and could represent up to fifty percent of the workforce. Some of the larger mines employed over two hundred and fifty children.

Cornish tin prices peaked and troughed throughout the 1800s, and periods of depression typically followed a drop in tin ore prices. The years of depression in tin mining during this period were: 1815 – 1821, together with parts of the 1840s (tin prices in 1843 were only 40% of what they were in 1810), 1860s, the late 1870s (following a boom in

1872) and 1890s. This cycle of boom and bust had predictable consequences. On a speaking engagement that brought John Wesley to Truro
on Tuesday, August 18, 1789, he noted in his journal: 'We went on to
Truro, where I had been appointed to preach at twelve o'clock; but here
an unforeseen hinderance occurred. I could not get through the main
street to our preaching-house. It was quite blocked up with soldiers
to the east, and numberless tinners to the west, a huge multitude of
whom, being nearly starved, were come to beg or demand an increase
in their wages, without which they could not live.' When mines closed,
poverty and social unrest followed as did the trend of miners emigrating
overseas to find new employment. Cornish miners travelled to America,
Australia, South Africa and the Far East in search of work and a new
life. This emigration out of Cornwall had two key effects, it depleted
the availability and capability of the Cornish mining industry and gave
impetus, knowledge and experience to foreign mining enterprises. In
time, both of these factors would have an impact on tin trading and the
ability of Cornish mines to compete with new mine fields. The success
of the early miners in their overseas ventures encouraged other miners
to leave Cornwall and find their fortunes elsewhere.

Other key factors impacted on the ability of tin mines to compete effectively on a world stage. As time went on, Cornish Mines were mining
deeper and deeper in search of ore. This had several consequences: the
time for miners to reach the mine face (often miles below the surface)
took longer, the time and effort to remove the ore from the mine face to
the surface took longer and involved costly transportation systems, the
cost of dewatering the mines and keeping them from flooding became
greater as the mines expanded and drove deeper.

When the mine owners and shareholders decided to suspend or close
a mine during periods of depressed tin and copper prices, the pumps

would be closed, and water would flood back into the tunnels and mine shafts. This happened to all deep mines whether or not the mine tunnels stretched under the sea. If the mine was reopened after the market recovered, then the first operation would be to pump out the water that had flooded into the mine. This pumping was extremely costly and time consuming, necessitating that any re-opening of an existing mine required a substantial amount of capital to finance the upfront remobilisation of activities, and pay for the pumping operations needed to make the mine workable again. This initial capital was effectively risked against the mine captain's last assessment from before the mine closed and before the ore become submerged under water. Sometimes the intervening period of closure could be years and many mines reopened and found that they were unable to produce a return sufficient to cover the initial and ongoing costs.

The cumbersome process of smelting and coinage set in place by the stannaries contributed to the cost of production and added a tax (coinage) that the overseas mines did not have to pay. Apart from the coinage, the tin ore from the mine had to be stored and later transported for smelting, After smelting, for which the mine paid, the metallic tin was stored again while awaiting transportation to the allotted coinage hall. Coinage only took place on certain stated days of the year and since the tin could not be sold until it was coined and stamped, this meant that the mine owners often had to wait for months before they could realise an income on their investment. This led to all sorts of side practices where the smelters would offer advances to the mines to facilitate immediate payment, but at a charge, or for a reduced payment of the ore's value. This added to the profits that the smelters made and in time the smelters acted almost as banks and gained control of several mining operations. The whole system was under pressure and in 1833 the stannaries agreed to amend the coinage system, but not abolish it. New coinage towns, including St Austell, were established and the frequency of coinage operations were increased. It was not until 1838 that coinage in Cornwall was finally abolished, allowing the Cornish tin mines to trade on an equitable basis with the rising overseas tin production.

The new tin mining operations in South America, Asia and Australia were often open cast mining, which was more efficient and less costly to mine than the deep mining taking place in Cornwall.

Over this period of time there were many external factors that had an impact on the mining industry. From 1789 Cornwall entered into a contract with the East India Company to supply up to twelve-hundred-tons of tin per year for export to China. The price agreed for each ton supplied was competitive and a law was passed that exempted this tin from tax, provided the location of import took the tin beyond the Cape of Good Hope. This contract continued over the next twenty-five years and helped during times of recession, but was resented during those times when the domestic tin price peaked and exceeded the contracted price with the East India Company. From 1812 the arrangement diminished and in time reversed when China and Asia started their own tin mining operations. As this Asian tin was produced at a lower cost than Cornish tin, imports to England started to impact the market.

The American Civil War from 1861 – 1865 led to a drop off in the requirement for tin plate, and by 1866 the price of Cornish tin had fallen one third since 1860. As a result of the price drop, numerous Cornish mines closed during the American Civil War years. This was a precursor to the peak of Cornish tin production in the 1870s when the war had concluded, demand picked up and supply had been reduced by the earlier closures.

There were also various gold rushes throughout the world during this period including Australia, South and North America, Africa, Canada and

New Zealand. These gold mines attracted skilled miners from Cornwall either as pioneers or to join other Cornish miners who were already overseas. Two former Australia prime ministers, Bob Hawke and Robert Menzies, traced their ancestry to Cornwall and there are many people of prominence in Canada and America (including Mark Twain aka Samuel Langhorne Clemens) who trace their ancestry back to Cornwall.

The conditions under which the mines operated were often squalid and unsafe. As mining shafts drove deeper the temperatures inside the mine could reach one hundred degrees Fahrenheit and up to one hundred percent humidity. This resulted in miners removing most of their clothes while they worked, as they were literally drenched in sweat. The lack of ventilation at depth combined to form a toxic atmosphere with dangerously high levels of carbon dioxide and dangerously low levels of oxygen. The use of black powder, and later dynamite, to open up new seams and the resultant dust and fumes would often exacerbate the situation. Over time the illnesses and fatalities associated with dust and ventilation in mines led to legislation and improvements.

Accidents were also prevalent, with falls being one of the major factors – from the moment a miner entered the mine the risk of trips and falls was significant. Access up and down the mines involved the use of ladders and stakes driven into the mine shafts and a slip could easily send a miner hurtling on a long fall down the shaft. The mine shaft ladders were often in poor condition as a result of damp conditions and material from the miners' boots adhering to the rungs. In addition, the ladder rungs were not always evenly spaced and were difficult to negotiate in semi-darkness. In the early days before electrification, the miners had to ascend and descend the mine shafts with only a candle to provide light.

The sub surface conditions proved a breeding ground for hookworm, an internal parasite that thrives in warm conditions. How it arrived here is unclear as it was not indigenous to Cornwall or Europe. Speculation at the time was that a miner returning from mining in India or the tropics brought the infection with him, and within the hot and humid conditions of the mine the hookworm spread. At Dolcoath mine in Cambourne, there was a severe outbreak and other mines and miners were similarly affected.

In his book 'Rambles Beyond Railways; Or Notes in Cornwall Taken A-Foot' published in 1851, the novelist Wilkie Collins gave an account of his visit to Botallack Mine on the north coast of the Land's End and Penwith Peninsula, near St Just:

Here the miner pulled up a trap-door and disclosed a perpendicular ladder leading down to a black hole, like the opening of a chimney. 'This is the shaft; I will go down first, to catch you in case you tumble; follow me and hold tight,' saying this, our friend squeezed himself through the trap-door, and we went after him as we had been bidden.

The black hole when we entered it, proved to be not quite so dark as it had appeared from above. Rays of light occasionally penetrated it through chinks in the outer rock. But by the time had got some little way further down, these rays began to fade. Then just as we seemed to be lowering ourselves into total darkness, we were desired to stand on a narrow landing-place opposite the ladder, and wait there while the miner went below for light. He soon reascended to us, bringing, not only the light he had promised, but a large lump of damp clay with it. Having lighted our candles he stuck them against the front of our hats with the clay – in order, as he said, to leave both our hands free to use as we liked . . .

The process of getting down the ladder was not very pleasant. They were all quite perpendicular, the rounds were placed at irregular distances, were many of them much worn away, and were slippery with water and copper-ooze. Add to this the narrowness of the shaft, the dripping wet rock shutting you in, as it were, all around your back and side against the ladder – the fathomless darkness beneath – the light flaring imme-diately above you, as if your head was on fire – the voice of the miner below, rumbling away in dull echoes lower and lower into the bowels of the earth – the consciousness that if the ladder broke you might fall down a thousand feet or so of tunnel in a moment – imagine all this, and you may easily realize what are the first impressions produced by a descent into a Cornish mine.

After emerging from the mine Wilkie Collins went on to record what their mining guide had to say:

'It's hard work we have to do, sir,' said my informant, summing up, when we parted, the propositions of good and evil in the social positions of his brethren and himself – 'harder work than people think, down in the heat and darkness underground. We may get a good deal at one time, but we get little enough at another; sometimes mines are shut up, and we are thrown out altogether – but, good work or bad work, or no work at all, what with our bits of ground for potatoes and greens, and what with cheap living, somehow we and our families make it do. We contrive to keep our good cloth coat for Sundays, and go to the chapel in the morning – for we're most of us Wesleyans – and then to church in the afternoon; so as to give 'em both their turn like! We never go near the mine on Sundays, except to look after the steam-pump: our rest, and our walk in the evening once a week, is a good deal to us. That's how we live, sir; whatever happens, we manage to work through and don't complain!'

It may seem incredulous to us in this day and age to know that the then revolutionary Metalliferous Mines Regulation Act of 1872 introduced regulations that prohibited women from working underground and set a minimum age of thirteen for boys to work underground. And even more surprising is that this law was met with opposition by some mines who had come to rely on younger, smaller boys, to squeeze into underground seams, shafts and tunnels.

One of the side benefits of the wealth coming from the mining in Cornwall at this time was the investment in high quality granite buildings and infrastructure, especially between 1850 – 1900. Still evident today are the streets and pavements of the larger towns, which are paved with dressed granite. It was from the 1840s that the major build of granite clad Wesleyan and Methodist Churches began, some fifty years after the death of John Wesley. And while this all pointed to a time of wealth for the county, it was in one respect the beginning of the end of mining in Cornwall. Thousands of years of mining had reached a crescendo in the nineteenth century only to falter and close by the end of it. From the 1870s many mines closed and were never to reopen again. Competition and the cost of deep mining saw the Cornish mining industry falter over the next half a century, to its virtual extinction by the 1930s. As a sign of how bad things were the Cornish smelters took to importing tin ore from abroad to smelt in their smelting houses.

The connection between Methodism and the mining industry in Cornwall is also significant. Since many miners were practising Methodists, the employment of Methodist lay preachers as mine captains was common and helped keep order and social discipline within the mines.

The 'Golden Age of Mining' was truly a turbulent phase of Cornish history. For the smelters it was a time of plenty, where they made money on the smelting operations and extended their reach into other aspects of the mining industry. For the mine owners and investors, fortunes were made or lost (or both) and for the populace, the extremes of life with and without employment rang the changes to the very fabric of their society. The effect of mine closures was felt at different times. Villages near profitable mines flourished while other villages suffered from these closures. The English historian A L Rowse described in his autobiography 'A Cornish Childhood' how villages and towns were very parochial, to the extent that they would not tolerate strangers in the village and were extremely protective of their own territory. There must have been great tension between these mining areas as unemployment and the need to find work brought miners from one district into another.

The modern-day Cornish buses carry an inscription and a picture of a Cornish Miner, abbreviated to the term Tinner. While this a great reminder of Cornwall's heritage, it would be a mistake to think of Cornwall as purely tin mining; it also mined copper, silver, arsenic, zinc, tungsten, lead and clay. William Gregor (1716 – 1817), a Cornish Clergyman and Mineralogist, is credited with discovering Titanium on the Lizard Peninsular in 1791.

REFLECTIONS

EFLECTING BACK ON THE PLACES and people in this area of West Cornwall has been intriguing and enlightening. For the people and characters who we have looked at in the preceding chapters, they come from their own place in time, and none of them have been able to do what we are now doing, looking back over centuries and millennia to see a fuller picture of history of West Cornwall. They saw a little, we can now see the whole, at least to our own point in time.

We have seen how the people grew, traded, developed, prospered, suffered, fought, sacrificed, lived and died over thousands of years. I find it amazing that we can still see objects and structures that these people would have seen. And while there are some unanswered questions, I have my own thoughts on the timelines. Looking back, I believe there was a highly organized civilisation living on the Land's End and Penwith Peninsula going back thousands of years BC. They built the ancient markers that we see today such as Men an Tol and Lanyon Quoit.

The rich and varied geology of Cornwall is part of its attraction as a place to live and to visit. It is the granite beneath Cornwall that has given rich veins of copper, tin and other metals. The colours, the texture and natural beauty of this granite are what give West Cornwall its distinct and rugged look, and of course gave Cornwall its mining heritage. I believe the people on the Land's End and Penwith Peninsula collaborated and worked together to establish the hill forts and promontory forts as they established their tin and copper trading during the Bronze Age and Iron Age.

It was fascinating when researching materials and places to find so many connections. Tregonning Hill, the location of our family holidays, I was to discover, was a castle fortress (Castle Pencair), the site of a Celtic settlement, a refuge for the Irish Missionary Saints, the site of discovery of China Clay, a mine which amongst others produced stone for Godolphin House and a site of celebration for the visits of Charles and John Wesley. The hill would have been familiar to the people I have written about in this book and those people from ancient times.

In closing my reflections I return to Tregonning Hill. The ancient and the modern meet within sight of Tregonning Hill and in the distance is the Goonhilly Satellite Earth Station. The first satellite dish went up in 1962 and Goonhilly went on to become the largest satellite station in the world. July 20, 2019, marked the fiftieth anniversary of the moon landings by Apollo 11, and part of the anniversary celebrations revisited the role played by Goonhilly in broadcasting the live coverage in the United Kingdom of those first moon steps. Goonhilly was once renowned for the horses and ponies bred and trained there and they were referred to as the Goonhilly nags or Goonhilly ponies. Goonhilly also has its own ancient monument close to the perimeter fence of the Earth Station, the Dry Tree Menhir is a three metre high standing stone, believed to be three-thousand-five-hundred years old.

When I drive by Tregonning Hill, my first thought is usually the holiday house, which I visited those many years ago, and then to reflect on all that has happened on that hill over the ages. It has been so rewarding to have found out more of the history for myself, although I know there are still more facts and stories that have been lost with time.

ANNEX

HOW PLACE NAMES HAVE CHANGED

- Mousehole was Moushal, Mowshole, Mowshall, Meddeshole, and in Cornish Port-ernis or Port inis

- Marazion was Mark. Jew or Market Jew, Marca-iewe, Maradzhawan, Maraz-Jowan, Marghas Yow, Marca-iewe, Markayowe.

- Penzance was Pensans.

- Zennor was Sener.

- St Ives was St Ithe or St Ithes or St Ies or St Ia.

- Morvah was Morvath.

- Loe Pool was the Pool or the low pool.

- Winnianton Farm was Wynnyton.

- Lizard Point was Lezard Poynt.

- Madron was Maderne, St Maderne.

- Mount's Bay was Mons Bay.

- Goldsithney was Goldsynnye.

- Land's End was Landes Ende.

- Sancreed was Santrete.

- Ludgvan was Ludgian.

- St Just was St Euste.

Some of these changes may be down to the spelling in old English, while some names have seen multiple changes.

ACKNOWLEDGEMENTS AND REFERENCES

The places mentioned in this work were visited and photographed by the author. A number of these locations had on site information, which was extremely helpful in providing research material.

The National Trust staff at Godolphin House and English Heritage staff at Chysauster Village.

Other useful information came from *I Walk Cornwall*, who have a circular navigated and narrated walk from Godolphin House, up Godolphin Hill, past the Great Work Mine, up Tregonning Hill, and back to Godolphin House. *I Walk Cornwall* also have a selection of walks all over Cornwall.

Ancestry.co.uk provided the platform to research information on a number of the families mentioned in the book.

IMAGE CREDITS

Map Marketing – © Map Marketing Ltd 2020. Map contains Ordnance Survey data © Crown Copyright and database 2020. Licence No: 100038862. All rights reserved. Reproduced by Permission of Map Marketing Ltd and Ordnance Survey.

Original antique map – courtesy of Jonathan Potter Ltd. G Van Keulen Map of Cornwall Published 1728 showing the Land's End and Penwith Peninsula, and the full extent of Mounts Bay to the Lizard Point. The map also identifies the location where the ship Presidents was lost at Loe Bar in 1684. Original antique map courtesy of Jonathan Potter Ltd.

Areas of Outstanding Natural Beauty – Copyright note included in map.

The Mining Districts of Cornwall – Copyright note included in map.

Cornubian Batholith: Granite Outcrops – Copyright note included in map.

Jospeph Mallord William Turner – Land's End – From Studies for Published 'England and Wales' Subjects, Land's End, Cornwall c.1834; Joseph Mallord William Turner 1775-1851; Photography credit of Photo © Tate.

St Michael's Mount: From Ivy Bridge to Penzance Sketchbook [Finberg CXXV] – St Michael's Mount, Marazion and Mount's Bay 1811; Joseph Mallord William Turner 1775-1851; Photography credit of Photo © Tate.

From Under the Sea, 1864 (oil on... Hook, James Clarke (1819-1907) – Credit: Manchester Art Gallery, UK/Bridgeman Images.

Francis Godolphin – ©National Trust Images.

Sidney Godolphin – © National Trust / Lynda Aiano.

The Godolphin Barb or The Godolphin Arabian (c. 1724–1753) with Grimalkin the Stable Cat (after George Stubbs after David Morier) – by David Morier (Berne 1705 – London 1770) © National Trust / Lynda Aiano.

St Michael's Mount – © National Trust Images/David Noton.

A view of the Crowns – © National Trust Images/John Miller.

Dollar Cove – © National Trust Images/John Miller.

Lanyon Quoit – © National Trust Images/Joe Cornish.

Author's Own Photos

A Cornish Dry-Stone Wall Showing a Rich Contrast in Colours

Sancreed Parish Church

The Strange Coloured Waters of a Cornish Clay Mine

Land's End, with the Longships Lighthouse in the Distance

Sir Humphrey Davy Statue in Penzance, Erected in 1872.

Men An Tol On The Land's End and Penwith Peninsula.

Clowance House, The Ancestral Home of the St Aubyn Family

Channels in the Sea at Mounts Bay

Tregonning Hill House

The Merry Maidens Stone Circle

BIBLIOGRAPHY

Speculi Britanniae Pars, A Topographical And Historical Description of Cornwall (1728), Author John Norden, Publisher Kessinger Publishing.

Observations on the antiquities historical and monumental, of the county of Cornwall, Author William Borlase, Publisher ECCO Print Editions.

Dr William Borlase, Rector of Ludgvan, dedicated his book 'Observations on the antiquities historical and monumental, of the county of Cornwall' to Sir John St Aubyn of Clowance. The two men were on cordial terms, although the families had been on different sides in the Civil War. The St Aubyns were parliamentarians and the Borlase family were royalists.

Cornwall in Prehistory, Author Toni-Maree Rowe, Publisher The History Press.

Victorian Maps Of England. The County and City Maps of Thomas Moule.

Ward Lock's Red Guide – West Cornwall and The Isles of Scilly.

Cornish Mines: St Just to Redruth. Author Barry Gamble. Publisher Alison Hodge.

The Geology and Landscape of Cornwall and the Isles of Scilly. Author Simon Camm. Publisher Alison Hodge.

A History of Tin Mining and Smelting in Cornwall, Author D.B. Barton, Publisher Cornwall Books.

Regulating Health and Safety in the British Mining Industries, 1800 – 1914, Author Catherine Mills, Publisher Ashgate Publishing and Routledge.

The Kings England CORNWALL, Author Arthur Mee, Publisher Hodder and Stoughton.

The History Of The Church In Paul Parish, Author G.M.Trelease. Publisher Aurelian Publishing.

The Journals of the Rev. John Wesley, A.M. Publisher The Epworth Press.

The Manuscript Journal of the Rev. Charles Wesley, M.A., S T Kimbrough Jr, Kenneth G C Newport. Publisher Kingswood.

Rambles Beyond Railways Or, Notes In Cornwall Taken a – Foot. Author Wilkie Collins, Publisher Richard Bentley.

A Book of Cornwall. Author S.Baring-Gould.

Cornish Characters And Strange Events. Author S.Baring-Gould.

Old Cornwall – Issued by The Federation of Old Cornwall Societies. Vol V No 10 1959.

The Story of the Cornish Language, Author Peter Berresford Ellis, Publisher Tor Mark Press.

A Cornish Childhood, Author A.L. Rowse, Publisher Jonathan Cape.

Penlee Lifeboat Station, Author Rachael Campey, Publishers RNLI.

Killers of the King, Author Charles Spencer, Publisher Bloomsbury.

To Catch a King, Author Charles Spencer, Publisher Bloomsbury.

The King's City, Author Don Jordan, Publisher Little, Brown.

Heroes of Cornwall, Author Sheila Bird, Publisher Countryside Books.

Ordnance Survey Explorer – Land's End Penzance & St Ives.

Dictionary of National Biography.

Chalmers General Biographical Dictionary.

Sherlock Holmes, His Last Bow – Sir Arthur Conan Doyle.

Leviathan – The Matter, Forme and Power of a Common-Wealth, Ecclesiastical and Civil – Thomas Hobbes.

The Bible NIV

Wikipedia.